digital Scrapbooking

THE CD-ROM IS LOCATED IN THE BACK OF THIS BOOK

THOMSON

COURSE TECHNOLOGY

Professional ■ Trade ■ Reference

digital Scrapbooking

cd included

Sally Beacham

Lori J. Davis

Important: Thomson Course Technology PTR cannot provide software support. Please contact the appropriate software manufacturer's technical support line or Web site for assistance.

Thomson Course Technology PTR and the author have attempted throughout this book to distinguish proprietary trademarks from descriptive terms by following the capitalization style used by the manufacturer.

Information contained in this book has been obtained by Thomson Course Technology PTR from sources believed to be reliable. However, because of the possibility of human or mechanical error by our sources, Thomson Course Technology PTR, or others, the Publisher does not guarantee the accuracy, adequacy, or completeness of any information and is not responsible for any errors or omissions or the results obtained from use of such information. Readers should be particularly aware of the fact that the Internet is an ever-changing entity. Some facts may have changed since this book went to press.

Educational facilities, companies, and organizations interested in multiple copies or licensing of this book should contact the publisher for quantity discount information. Training manuals, CD-ROMs, and portions of this book are also available individually or can be tailored for specific needs.

ISBN: 1-59200-503-9

Library of Congress Catalog Card Number: 2004106602

Printed in the United States of America

04 05 06 07 08 BU 10 9 8 7 6 5 4 3 2 1

THOMSON

™

COURSE TECHNOLOGY

Professional ■ Trade ■ Reference

Thomson Course Technology PTR,
a division of Thomson Course Technology
25 Thomson Place
Boston, MA 02210
http://www.courseptr.com

SVP, Thomson Course Technology PTR:
Andy Shafran

Publisher:
Stacy L. Hiquet

Senior Marketing Manager:
Sarah O'Donnell

Marketing Manager:
Heather Hurley

Manager of Editorial Services:
Heather Talbot

Senior Acquisitions Editor:
Kevin Harreld

Senior Editor:
Mark Garvey

Associate Marketing Managers:
Kristin Eisenzopf
and Sarah Dubois

Project Editor/Copy Editor:
Kelli Crump Weiner

Technical Reviewer:
Angela M. Cable

Course Technology PTR Market Coordinator:
Amanda Weaver

Interior Layout Tech:
Marian Hartsough

Cover Designer:
Mike Tanamachi

CD-ROM Producer:
Brandon Penticuff

Indexer:
Katherine V. Stimson

Proofreader:
Sara Gullion

"Where Mother Is"

PHYLLIS SUSAN RAND BRADBURY   and   BARBARA ANN RUST DAVIS

July 10, 1924 – May 23, 2004   November 21, 1935 – December 6, 2002

This book is dedicated to memories
of the hearts and spirits of our mothers

Acknowledgments

As any good scrapbooker knows, photos provide the foundation for our memories, but words tell the story. We'd like to acknowledge the help, support, direction, attention, affection, love, hot food, and cold beverages, as well as oceans of coffee, provided to us by our loved ones, friends, editors, and scrapbook lovers throughout the land.

In particular, the Beacham-Lachance-Dunham clan and the Davis-Synal family—thank you John and Larry, the best in-house tech support anyone could ask for (heavy on the support, low on the tech!). To our assorted family members and friends who appear throughout this book—feel the love. Wade, Emilie and Brittanie—thanks for being accommodating as well as photogenic.

Thanks to our editors Kevin Harreld and Kelli Crump. Great ideas, great "red pencil". We'd like to thank our technical editor, Angela Cable, who also contributed CD resources, as well as our favorite supplier of fabulous photographs, Darth Vector himself, Ron Lacey.

The folks at Digital Scrapbook Place deserve special thanks, particularly owner/designers Margie Lundy and Amanda Behrmann, as well as designers Lauren Bavin, Kim Liddiard, and Jenna Robertson. We'd also like to thank Janice "Maya" Dye-Szucs and Tracy Pori for their contributions to our CD resources. Special thanks to Ray Larabie, Ronna Penner, and House of Lime for some fabulous fonts—please visit the sites listed in the book's Appendix A to see more work from these terrific designers.

Many scrapbook designers, both paper and digital, contributed artwork for this book. We'd like to thank Jenny Bamford-Perkins, Kristin Cronin-Barrow, Pat Goettels, Jeri Ingalls, and Samuel Kordik. Very special thanks go to Cindi Bisson for guiding (and bearing with!) Sally through her head-long rush into paper scrapbooking, and to Sandi Ducote for dragging Sally kicking and screaming into digital scrapbooking. Without her, this book would never have come to be.

Thanks to all the software developers who contributed demos and other resources for our book's CD: Harald Heim of The Plugin Site; Amedeo Rosa at Alien Skin Software; Edie McRee at Auto F/X; Alex Shalikashvili; Kohan Ikin; Ilya Razmanov; John Redfield; Joe Donnelly at Hemera; Michael Sheasby at LumaPix; Aaron Epstein at Color Schemer; Virtual Painter; and Dover Publications.

We'd like to acknowledge, thank, and generally recognize their excellence as friends, pals, inspiration and/or partners in crime: Gary Barton, Patricia "Porter" Caldwell, Joe Fromm, Jeanmarie "JP" Kabala, Jackie Laderoute, Nancy Peterson, Kerry Pierce, Bill Schnakenberg, Tom Vallombroso, Beth Winter, and Kris Zaklika. Also, Vikki Brooks, Phyllis List, Jerry O'Brien, Sonja Shea, and Barbara Wallis, as well as Channen McGhee, Norene Malaney, Mei Liu, and the Knezevich clan.

Sally would like to thank Lori for helping her do battle with Word . . . and Lori would like to thank Sally for enabling her to max out her credit card at the scrapbook store, if only Larry would let her.

Last but not least, we'd like to acknowledge the contributions of our favorite non-human friends: kitties Little Max, Lucas, Einstein, and Moussie; the incomparable Bijou the Alaskan Husky; Bob the Bobcat; and the Chipmunks of Northern Ontario.

About the Authors

SALLY BEACHAM is an author and teacher, specializing in Paint Shop Pro, Photoshop-compatible plug-in filters, and digital scrapbook design. She teaches a series of classes at www.lvsonline.com and develops tutorials and resources for plug-in filters at www.dizteq.com. Sally lives in southern Maine with her husband, John, and assorted children and cats.

LORI J. DAVIS is a technical writer and author of several books on Paint Shop Pro. She is a computer graphics fanatic, with a love for exploring the ins and outs of image editors and plug-in filters. She has taught numerous online courses and has a popular graphics-related Web site, Lori's Web Graphics, at loriweb.pair.com. She enjoys photography, crafts, painting, gardening—all with "help" from her two cats—and walking on the beach with her husband, Larry.

Contents at a Glance

Contents

3

Basic Layout Guidelines   51

4

Adding Graphic Elements 75

5

Text Techniques 99

6

Enhancing Your Pages with Filters 125

7

Advanced Photo Techniques 145

8

9

10

Further Fun with Photos   219

A

Resources   245

Index   257

Introduction

*S*crapbooking, the art of creating personal memory pages from photos, memorabilia, and ornamentation, is a trend with explosive growth. *Digital scrapbooking* is the process of creating most or all of a memory page on a computer.

Digital scrapbooking can be as easy or complex as you like. You can quickly assemble entire albums using premade digital components, and your own photos, or you can make everything from scratch, taking pleasure in the art of creation. There's no mess, no worries about storage of tools and supplies, and the process is generally much less expensive than traditional paper scrapbooking.

Digital scrapbooking appeals to a wide variety of users. If you've got a digital camera, you've probably found yourself with many more photos than you might have previously had from a traditional camera. This allows you lots of room to experiment, but what do you do with them? Digital scrapbooking can provide another creative outlet to make good use of those personal photos.

Heritage photos, those vintage and antique photos we all yearn to inherit, can be organized through digital scrapbooking in a meaningful fashion, repaired as needed, and shared with all family members who might also want copies. You can experiment all you want on scanned copies, and archive the originals safely for future generations.

Overloaded with children's school and activity photos, artwork, and other memorabilia? Scan them in, turn them into digital scrapbook layouts, and store the originals.

It's interesting to see who produces digital scrapbooks. Here are a few examples of digital scrappers who contributed to this book.

We have layouts from a teenage boy from the United States, Samuel Kordik, who scrapbooks his own life and that of his family.

There are photos and "photo essays" from Ron Lacey, an author/teacher/photographer from Ontario, Canada, who doesn't do "traditional scrapbooking," but creates digital photographic memories incorporating text as journaling.

When I made my first iced Chai, all my brothers wanted to try it! I let them eac have one sip, and they loved it so much that they were helping me out all over the place, hoping to get one of their own.
Later, when I had completed most of my homework, I helped them make their own, and they were extremely grateful.
Iced Chai is a thick, rich and cold beverage with the full taste of spicy Chai tea. It really goes well with the fresh excitement of Spring.

"My Chai" is a computer-generated scrapbook layout by Samuel Kordik.

Split Rock Lighthouse
Located on the north Shore of Lake Superior this lighthouse was built in 1910. Due to the extreme depths close to the shoreline, sounding to maintain a safe distance from the rocky coast is difficult. This along with the large iron ore deposits in the area creating erratic compass readings were the main reasons for the construction of the Split Rock Liight. Prior to it's construction there were several shipwrecks in foggy weather. A few hundred feet from the light lies the wreck of the Madeira (inset), a steel hulled schooner barge that went down in the great gail of 1905 which was the cause of over 30 wrecks on Lake Superior.

The lighthouse was decommisioned in 1969 but is now the centerpiece of a state park and, in memory of the wreck of the Edmund Fitzgerald, it is lit once a year on the anniversary of the sinking.

©2004
Ron Lacey

"Split Rock Lighthouse" layout by Ron Lacey.

We also have layouts and CD resources from Lauren Bavin, a stay-at-home mom from New Zealand, who has taken to digital scrapbooking with a passion. Lauren focuses on her three children and creates realistic digital scrapbook elements for her personal use, which are avidly sought by other digital scrapbookers for their own pages.

"Sk8rboy" is a computer-generated scrapbook layout by Lauren Bavin, featuring digital elements on this book's resource CD.

There are many other folks from around the world who have discovered the fun and satisfaction of digital scrapbooking. As is common with magazines devoted to traditional scrapbooking, we've used exciting page designs and creations from a number of designers throughout the book and on the resource CD.

What You'll Find in This Book

This book provides information on what digital scrapbooking is along with techniques for creating your own digital scrapbooks. There are also chapters on digital photography and methods for creating your own digital scrapbook elements.

Who This Book Is For

This book is for anyone who wants to learn about digital scrapbooking and create their own digital layouts. Some will have experience with paper scrapbooking and some will not. Some will have experience with digital photography and some will not. Some want to create their own scrapbook elements and some want to create layouts from ready-made layout kits.

This book assumes only that you have basic knowledge of computing and that you have an image editor, such as Digital Image Pro, Paint Shop Pro, PhotoImpact, or Photoshop Elements, and have mastered the fundamentals of how to use it.

How This Book Is Organized

The book contains 10 chapters, one appendix, and a resource CD:

- **Chapter 1, Scrapbooking Why and How.** Understanding basic scrapbook concepts. Pros and cons of paper and digital scrapbooking. Hardware, software, and tools necessary or desirable to scrapbook digitally.
- **Chapter 2, Digital Photo Fundamentals.** Information on digital photography and scanning, and basic photo editing techniques such as rotating, cropping, and resizing; automatic color and contrast correction; blurring and sharpening; and noise reduction.
- **Chapter 3, Basic Layout Guidelines.** Choosing the optimal size of scrapbook layouts. Examples of layout designs and styles. Creating basic layouts in popular image editors. Choosing color schemes. Adding textures and photos.
- **Chapter 4, Adding Graphic Elements.** Adding photos, mats, frames, and borders. Creating edge effects. Colorizing existing elements. Adding tags and banners.

- **Chapter 5, Text Techniques.** How to add and modify text, where to find fonts, and what you can do to create beautiful text effects.

- **Chapter 6, Enhancing Your Pages with Filters.** How to use plug-in filters to create great effects for your layouts.

- **Chapter 7, Advanced Photo Techniques.** More photo techniques, including cropping, manual color correction, and converting color photos to black and white.

- **Chapter 8, Sharing Your Work.** Ideas and techniques for sharing your digital layouts in print, online, and on digital media.

- **Chapter 9, Creating Your Own Elements.** Techniques for creating your own digital background papers, frames, brads, eyelets, and more.

- **Chapter 10, Further Fun with Photos.** Fun things to do with the photos you use in your layouts, including compositing, tinting and colorizing, using photos as the basis of digital drawings and paintings, and creating panoramas.

- **Appendix A, Resources.** Online resources for scrapbooking, image editors, and graphics tools, photography, and scanning.

What's on the CD

This book also includes a resource CD with supplementary information, examples, and tools. The CD is divided into six sections:

- **Tutorials.** Several application-specific tutorials for Digital Image Pro 9, Paint Shop Pro 8.1, PhotoImpact XL, PhotoPlus 9, and Photoshop Elements 2.0. You can find this content in the \Tutorials folder on the CD.

- **Kits and Elements.** Kits, templates, and alphabets from well-known digital scrapbook designers. You can find this content in the \Kits_and_Elements folder on the CD.

- **Fonts.** Over 100 fonts from highly-regarded font designers. You can find this content in the \Fonts folder on the CD.

- **Clip Art.** Clip art samples from Dover Publications and Hemera. You can find this content in the \ClipArt folder on the CD.

- **Plug-ins and Utilities.** Free and shareware plug-in filters, demo filters, and utilities. You can find this content in the \Plugins_and_Utilities folder on the CD.

- **Sample Layouts.** Layouts featured in the book and in the kits and templates offered on the CD. You can find this content in the \SampleLayouts folder on the CD.

Digital
Scrapbooking

1

Scrapbooking Why and How

Welcome to the wondrous world of digital scrapbooking. This is a world populated with computers and cameras, pixels, and printers—all devoted to helping you preserve memories in a style and format that suits your needs. We'll be your guides as you travel through the world of computer-generated memory page construction.

The Scrapbooking Concept

What's a scrapbook? Why scrapbook? Who scrapbooks? Why use a computer to help scrapbook?

All excellent questions—let's start with "What's a scrapbook?" For countless generations, people have documented life's experiences by saving memorabilia and photographs in albums for themselves and others to enjoy. Often these pages include decorative accents and text called *journaling* by scrapbookers. Traditionally, these pages, also known as *layouts*, are stored in albums of many sizes and types.

Scrapbooking is a very personal concept, and some consider it personal art. It's also flexible, and encompasses a multitude of techniques, both artistic and craft-oriented. Scrapbooking encourages even the most inexperienced photographer to create beautiful and meaningful arrangements, and challenges the experienced designer to make some magic.

Some scrapbooks have themes, such as weddings or a new baby. Some scrapbooks document events; an entire scrapbook devoted to a cruise vacation. In Figure 1.1, notice the

Figure 1.1 Computer-generated scrapbook layouts by Lauren Bavin, Amanda Behrman, Jeri Ingalls, and Margie Lundy.

layout examples celebrating everyday events, sports, and friendships. Heritage scrapbooks are popular. These are journals that record genealogical information and incorporate family pictures, sometimes with antique photos as well as period memorabilia.

Creating a scrapbook can be a relaxing hobby, an interesting avocation, and an important record of past and current history for future generations. Many scrapbookers enjoy meeting for communal events called *crops*—a reference to cropping photographs to fit the available layout space. Scrapbooking is popular in many countries, although supply sources may be somewhat limited. Sometimes the communal events involve using Web forums, e-mail lists, and chat applications.

It's become increasingly popular to use computers to assist in creating scrapbooks. The simplest form is creating journaling and heading banners. The sheer variety of available fonts makes this task not only easy, but extremely flexible. However, today's scrapbooker can go as far as to create entire layouts from start to finish with a computer and various types of software. It's also easy to print the entire layout in one fell swoop, or save it to a CD-ROM for storage purposes or to share with others. Sometimes, layouts are shared via Web galleries, as shown in Figure 1.2, or personal Web sites as well.

Figure 1.2 Member Gallery at www.digitalscrapbookplace.com, courtesy Sandi Ducote.

Traditional Paper Scrapbooks

Paper scrapbook pages can be created in a variety of sizes, and more styles than one can even imagine. Commonly, a scrapbook layout is placed in a plastic sleeve protector to help safeguard it from dust, dirt, and fingerprints (people *do* actually look at their scrapbooks). The sleeve protectors are stored in an album, oftentimes with a decorative cover. The paper layout in Figure 1.3 is designed as a 12 × 12 inch cardstock-mounted layout.

Figure 1.3 Traditional paper layout, courtesy Cynthia Bisson.

Albums can be purchased in a variety of sizes. Most often, you'll find 12 × 12 inch and 8.5 × 11 inch (the dimensions of the paper layouts, not necessarily the external dimensions of the book itself). Other available sizes include 12 × 15 inch, 8 × 8 inch, 6 × 6 inch, and 5 × 7 inch. You can even create your own custom size using a binding machine.

The album binding itself is also a variable. The most popular binding types are strap-hinge (a metal strap goes through holes in the pages and the binding) and post-bound (expandable metal posts create the binding.) Page protectors usually are *top-loading*—the layout is inserted from the top of the sleeve, making it more difficult for attachments to fall out of the protector if they become dislodged. If you choose to create digital layouts and print them out, you can still use the same types of albums and page protectors to showcase them.

Journals and Altered Books

There are a number of variations on the scrapbook concept. A couple of those are journals and altered books. A *journal* is a scrapbook that concentrates on the text aspect; it still incorporates photos and images, but generally tells a cohesive story from beginning to end. Journals are easy for the digital scrapper to create—all it takes is a word processor and some clip art.

Altered books are actual books that become the bound medium for collage-style scrapbooking. You can find them at second-hand stores, yard sales, and flea markets. Sometimes the book itself is an intrinsic part of the scrapbook theme, as shown in Figure 1.4.

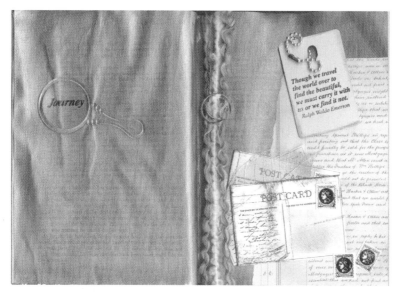

Figure 1.4 Altered book, courtesy Jenny Bamford-Perkins.

The altered book format can be an interesting way to display computer-generated scrap-book art.

Paper vs. Digital Scrapbooking

What are the advantages of each type of scrapbooking? What do you need to start digital scrapbooking, what's it going to cost, and how does it compare to traditional paper scrapbooking?

Pros and Cons

Digital scrapbooking has a number of significant advantages over paper-based scrapbooking (see Figure 1.5). The disadvantages comprise a short list, so let's start with those:

- Paper scrapbookers love the feel of handling components, and the process of physically creating artwork with their hands and tools. That "hands-on" feel doesn't seem quite the same when you're "cutting and pasting" with a mouse.

- Digital scrapbooking doesn't require as many tools and accessories, but the tools you do need are major purchases—printers, scanners, and computers!

- If you have no background knowledge, it's not as fast and easy to learn how to produce an effect on a computer as it is to learn to cut a paper shape or layer paper for a layout. The learning curve is much steeper.

Figure 1.5 Traditional paper layout, courtesy Pat Goettel.

On the other hand, the advantages are countless:

- Since many of us already own most of the hardware and a lot of the necessary software for digital scrapbooking, it can be a much less expensive way to document memories. Paper scrapbooking tools and supplies can be expensive, and you need a lot of them.

- Digital resources are infinitely reusable. Once you use a package of "real" eyelets, they're gone and you must buy more. One computer-generated image of an eyelet can be used over and over, and modified in size and color to match any design scheme.

- Storage space! Finding storage space for all those paper scrapbooking supplies is a major undertaking—if you don't have a separate craft area or room, your family might find the dining room table overrun with scrapbook tools. Digital scrappers keep all their supplies and works in progress on computer media storage, just like any other data file. The work area is confined to the computer area, which may already be an integral part of your home's design.

- Digital scrapbooking is flexible. Layouts can quickly be changed in size, design scheme, and color. Try doing that with paper.

- Once you're familiar with the software, you can work quickly. And, you can create multiple copies at the same time—so if you want to create a theme scrapbook for yourself, and other family members decide they want one too, you can print all of them together.

- Creating layouts digitally removes much of the necessity for maintaining strict archival-quality standards for photos. Since you're always working with a digital copy and not an original, another copy can be generated in seconds should something happen to the first one.

- Digital photos can be edited (usually in the same software you use to create the layout) saving time as well as allowing you to correct and enhance photos and even create special effects.

- Computer-generated layouts can be archived as data files to preserve copies or to print at a later date. They can be created as Web graphics for display on a Web site or gallery, or burned to a CD for viewing. They can also be sent via e-mail to far-away friends and family.

Using a computer to enhance and create scrapbooking can be as simple or complex as you would like. Sometimes, you might just add computer-generated journaling and title banners to paper layouts to compensate for poor handwriting, or to make use of the thousands of terrific font types and styles, many of them free on the Internet. In Figure 1.6, the artist used text as an integral part of the layout design.

Figure 1.6 "Believe in Magic" by Lauren Bavin.

Other ways you can add digital components to your scrapbooking is to create your own clip art to use as stickers and shapes and realistic-looking embellishments, all without adding bulk to your pages.

NOTE

> Digital scrapbooking has a language and terminology all its own. The popular paper scrapbook term for decorative objects added to a paper layout is embellishments. Digital scrappers refer to computer-generated embellishments as elements. We'll also use this term in the book, but don't confuse it with the software application Photoshop Elements, which will also be covered.

Sometimes, digital scrapbookers design page layouts that leave space for photos to be added after the layout is printed. This is useful if you're creating gift albums for someone else, and don't have the actual pictures that will be included. Perhaps a new baby is on its way, but not yet here. You can make an album of pre-constructed pages and present it as a shower gift, before Junior even arrives.

Of course, if you'd like to create a totally digital page, you can do that too, with the entire layout created on the computer, including the photos, which can be digitally corrected and enhanced, cropped, and sized to fit your page perfectly. Then the layout can be printed as is, stored for later printing, archived, resized for display in a Web gallery, or sent through e-mail. Once the layout is constructed, it's a simple matter to create many types of media from it.

Tools of the Trade

You'll need a computer to create digital scrapbook pages and software. In this book, we'll use a number of different applications to show you how to create digital layouts. It's not the tools that you use, it's what you do with the tools (although some are more flexible and full-featured than others).

Most often, digital scrapbookers use image editors such as Photoshop, Photoshop Elements, Paint Shop Pro, Digital Image Pro, PhotoImpact, and PhotoPlus to create entire layouts. It's also possible to use drawing programs like Illustrator, CorelDRAW, and Xara X to do this as well as page layout programs like PagePlus. Word-processing applications like Word and desktop publishers such as Publisher can be used as well. Each of these types of applications has its own advantages and disadvantages.

Image editors excel at working with photographs, and scrapbooks are about photographs primarily. Figure 1.7 shows photos ready to edit in Serif's PhotoPlus 9. Paint programs such as this sometimes balk at large file sizes and digital layouts prepared for print tend to be large files. Another advantage to using an image editor/paint program is there are lots of third-party plug-in filters that allow the user to easily create special effects. We'll show you how some of those work in a later chapter.

Drawing applications like Illustrator are great for creating your own page elements, but they don't work so well for photo editing. Page layout, desktop publishing, and word-processing programs are all well-suited for print results and generally handle large file sizes, but don't usually have the tools and features that allow the digital scrapper to edit photos and create custom embellishments. There's no one "do-it-all" program for digital scrapbookers, so we'll cover paint program-type image editors in this book as well.

What Does Scrapping Cost?

We've already mentioned that digital scrapbook resources are reusable—create or purchase a computer-generated embellishment and it's yours forever, to modify as you like to use in as many layouts as you want.

Figure 1.7 Editing photos in PhotoPlus.

Perhaps you wonder how much it will cost to create your own digital scrapbooks. The short answer is *a lot* less than paper scrapbooks of the same design and complexity. You probably already own a computer, but you might want to add some additional RAM memory, as scrapping with a paint program requires quite a bit of memory resources. (Anything over 512 MB of RAM should be adequate, but the sky's the limit when it comes to memory, the more the merrier.)

There are two areas where you are likely to spend some money: software to produce your layouts and the method you use to print them. We'll discuss software and inkjet printers later, but let's devote some time to printing methods now.

If you don't want to print your layouts at home, other options include having them printed by a photo-finisher, in which case you'll want to design your layouts in a common photo print size, such as 8 × 10 inch. You can also have layouts printed by office supply and copy shops, as a color photocopy. Generally, the largest size that can be economically printed is on 11 × 14 inch paper, which means using a standard paper size of 11 × 17 inches and trimming it. Then you can mount the layout on regular 12 × 12 inch cardstock sheets for placement in an album.

Of course, you don't have to print digital layouts at all. You can choose to store and view them as digital images, perhaps burned to CD-ROM for easy viewing, which is a cheap and portable way to store them. If you go this route, you might want to use a slide-show program like PowerPoint to present the layouts. Some of these applications can even incorporate music and sound files.

Layouts can also be shown in Web galleries and on personal Web sites. Many of the digital scrapbook resource sites include picture galleries where members can display their scrapbook layouts:

- www.digitalscrapbookplace.com
- www.scrapbook-bytes.com
- www.pagesoftheheart.net

You'll find lots of resources for digital scrappers (as well as some paper scrapbook information) at these sites, from free embellishments and paper downloads to chat forums for live interaction with other scrapbookers.

Digital Scrapbook Necessities and Niceties

Items such as computers and software are necessities for digital scrapbooking, but there are lots of other "nice-to-have's" that can make the digital scrapbook process easier, more fun, and flexible.

Hardware and Peripherals

Computer hardware types abound, almost all of it useful for digital scrapbooking. It's not necessary to have or use all the types presented, but each peripheral adds another dimension to your ability to scrapbook.

Scanners

A scanner is handy to have, as most photos came into existence long before the days of consumer digital cameras. Scanning in old photos provides a nearly instantaneous means to archive precious and unique photos as well as multiple copies for many uses. You can have this done professionally, but it's fairly expensive and less convenient than scanning in your home at a moment's notice.

You'll probably find the most useful type of scanner is the flatbed type. Most consumer-level scanners will handle up to 8.5 × 11 inch paper or photos. There are scanners available with larger scanning beds, but they are generally much more expensive. If you need to scan in a larger document or object, you can always scan it in sections and then "stitch" the sections together using your graphics application or panorama-stitching software.

Not only is a scanner handy for photos, but it's also great for creating your own background papers and pattern fills. You can lay leaves or flowers directly on the scanner bed and cover with a white or black cloth. Even pocket change can become an interesting background image, as shown in Figure 1.8. If you want to scan something you fear may scratch the scanner bed, try laying a piece of clear film, such as an overhead transparency sheet, over the bed and then laying down your objects. You can use a clear Pyrex baking dish for messy items, even liquids. You won't be able to close the scanner lid, so cover this dish with a cloth before scanning.

You might find a dedicated slider scanner useful, like the one shown in Figure 1.9, if you have lots of old slides. Many flatbed scanners also include a slide scanner attachment. www.dpreview.com is a useful Web site for product information and reviews on scanners and digital cameras.

Figure 1.8 Scanning objects on a flatbed scanner, courtesy Ron Lacey.

Figure 1.9 Slide scanner, camera, and slides, courtesy Ron Lacey.

Printer

A printer is almost a must-have for a digital scrapbooker. Printers can be used to print photos, layout elements, or entire pages. If you want a mostly traditional paper layout, you can print journaling blocks and page titles only. It's possible to create your own text and photo transparency sheets. In addition, you can print background papers — printing directly on textures like fabric and cork, if it's thin enough for your printer. Delicate fabrics, tissue paper and gauze can even be printed, by first ironing them to ordinary freezer paper (the kind you buy in a roll like aluminum foil) and then cutting to fit the printer's paper tray. You can also use adhesive to adhere small tags and titles to a full-size paper sheet, and send it through the printer. You'll be able to lift the smaller paper piece off the full-size sheet and adhere it to your layout.

The most convenient means of printing your digital layouts is a home-based inkjet printer. You may already have one, and if it's a photo-quality printer, that's even better. If you're interested in buying a printer specifically to print your digital layouts, keep the following information in mind:

■ Printed output can only be as good as the printer that produces it. A printer capable of higher print resolution—measured in ink dots per inch, or DPI—will produce a better quality image than one that's only capable of a lower DPI.

- Some printers use special pigment inks and compatible papers to produce photos and layouts that are rated as fade-resistant for many years (sometimes up to 200 years!). While we don't have to maintain strict archival standards for our photos when working with computer-generated layouts, it's good to know that an album can still be expected to be in good condition when our grandchildren pull it out of the attic. If this is a concern to you, look for a printer that uses pigment inks and be sure to use the paper and ink recommended by the printer manufacturer for the longest possible expected life of your layouts.

- Many inkjet printers can only print up to 8.5 × 11 inch layouts, and sometimes not even that size if the printer isn't capable of borderless (full-bleed) printing. If you're interested in printing l2 × 12 inch layouts, you'll need a wide-format printer that can handle up to 13 × 19 inch paper. There are several models of printers available that meet that requirement, in several price ranges.

Digital scrapbookers often choose to design layouts for 8 × 10 inches; they can be easily printed on a home inkjet printer, or can be printed by a photo developer, with no size adjustments.

The layout in Figure 1.10 was printed on a wide-format printer, the Hewlett Packard 9650, on 13 × 19 semi-gloss photo paper. One 12 × 12 inch copy and two 6 × 6 inch copies were produced on each sheet, resulting in layouts for three separate albums, at an average cost of under $1.00 for each layout for ink and paper consumables. Paper and ink prices vary widely, so look for a good balance of cost vs. quality.

Figure 1.10 "Bijou and Bob" digital layout by Sally Beacham.

Photo Printer

You may want a photo printer, in addition to or instead of, a regular inkjet printer. Many photo printers use special pigment inks, which have archival qualities better than photographs developed commercially. Figure 1.11 shows a wide-format printer that uses pigment inks, capable of producing prints as large as 13 inches wide (and can also use roll paper with a special attachment). Some printers that use dye-based inks can produce photos and layouts with life expectancies of 30 years or more.

Archival life ratings are usually based on using the recommended ink and paper from the printer manufacturer. If the manufacturer offers different types of paper, check to see for which ink types it's suited. For example, Epson makes several types of pigment and dye inks and paper suited to one ink or the other.

NOTE

Most testing to evaluate archival properties is done simulating exposure to ultraviolet light under glass—as if a photo was hung on a wall in a room with normal daylight. Most scrapbook layouts are actually stored in archival-safe plastic sleeves in albums, so they will probably last much longer than the rated life.

Figure 1.11 Epson 2200 wide-format photo printer, photo courtesy Ron Lacey.

You can also choose from different paper finishes—matte, glossy, and semi-gloss paper. The finish best for your scrapbook layouts is purely a matter of personal preference. Many new printers come with a sample pack of papers. Try them to help you determine which you like best.

Digital Cameras

Where would digital scrapbooking be without digital cameras? The price and availability of digital cameras has allowed the home user to produce excellent images in a jiffy, and that's opened the door for designing beautiful and expressive layouts on the computer as well. A digital camera is perhaps a scrapbooker's favorite tool—without photos, there's nothing to scrapbook (see Figure 1.12).

A digital camera is also helpful for the same reason as a scanner—you can create your own customized papers and embellishments from objects around you. Everyone's garden yields great grasses, ferns, leaves, and blossoms that you can use to decorate a page.

Figure 1.12 "Nature Photography with Canon Pro90" by Ron Lacey.

Everyday objects, such as the detail of an old stone bridge, as shown in Figure 1.13, can be photographed and used as decorative elements. Even interesting surfaces can quickly become your new background paper—think rust, cement, and peeling paint.

Depending on your budget and skill level, you can find a camera to meet most any need. Cameras by all the top manufacturers are similar in price and features, so try out several models before you choose.

TIP

How many megapixels do you need? Scrapbookers tend to use smaller snapshot-size photos in their layouts, so you may not need as many megapixels as you think. On the other hand, don't shut out the possibility of using and printing larger photos, and cropping out interesting details. A good rule of thumb for superior print quality:

2 megapixels = 4 × 6 or snapshot size

3 megapixels = 5 × 7

4 megapixels = 8 × 10

5 megapixels = 11 × 14

Figure 1.13 Photo of Boston bridge detail.

Some important features to consider when you're buying a camera:

- **Camera image format.** Does it store the images in a proprietary format, such as a RAW file, and if so, is software included to convert those files to more common file formats?
- **Image quality.** Are there various quality level settings to balance file size vs. image size?
- **Storage media.** What type and size is included with the camera? Practically no camera comes with adequate storage media, so you'll definitely need more.
- **Zoom capabilities.** Optical zoom good, digital zoom bad! Digital zoom is the equivalent of zooming and cropping in a graphics application. It doesn't add any pixels or better quality to the image you're viewing.
- **Battery type.** Proprietary? Rechargeable? Wouldn't be good to be stuck in the middle of nowhere looking at the photo opportunity of a lifetime and your battery dies, with no backup battery and no hope of using widely-available AA batteries.

Graphics Tablet

Many people find a graphics tablet useful. This is a digitizing device that functions like a mouse and allows you to use a stylus to draw or write on a tablet surface. A graphics tablet can be a more natural method of drawing, but it does take a little practice to use it. If you're interested in learning more about graphics tablets, check out Wacom, the leading manufacturer of graphics tablets. Their Graphire line is less expensive than the Intuos line, and is a good choice for a novice artist. More information on Wacom's line of graphics tablets can be found at www.wacom.com.

Software

We've already mentioned some common types of software that the digital scrapbooker may find useful. Here we'll go into a bit more detail on what's currently available, and what we'll focus on in this book.

Useful Application Types

Many people begin digital scrapbooking by using a card-creator or print shop program. These applications often have special scrapbook templates built right in. They generally have some clip art included, and can be a good introductory program. You'll probably outgrow them quickly; they're usually quite limited in their flexibility.

Some companies offer special scrapbook creation applications. They also often have lots of included clip art, but tend to be limited in tools and features and don't "grow" with the user. They do include lots of layout templates, so it might be worthwhile to investigate and learn good design tips. The art choices tend to be cartoonish, cutesy, or feminine. If these styles don't appeal to you—look elsewhere.

Painting applications such as Paint Shop Pro and Photoshop Elements are the most common choice for digital scrapbooking. Paint programs are usually distinguished by the ability to handle photographs well, and to create new images using brush tools. Most advanced paint programs have features like image layers and the ability to use selections, masks, and special effects (more on all of this much later).

Photoshop is the mother of all paint applications, but it's also very expensive and difficult to learn. Almost any mid-price paint application contains enough tools and features to let the digital scrapbooker create anything they like—they are usually a tenth of the cost of Photoshop. For this reason, we won't cover it in this book.

Paint Shop Pro, Photoshop Elements, PhotoImpact, PhotoPaint, and PhotoPlus all have similar features—some work better or more easily than others, but all essentially can create the same layout. Microsoft's Digital Image Pro is very popular. It's good for photos, but has no real layers and lacks some essential tools for scrapbooking.

Illustration software, such as Xara X, Illustrator, and CorelDRAW, are good choices if you would like to create your own embellishments from scratch. Illustration programs are considered "drawing" applications vs. the "paint" applications previously mentioned. We won't work with these types of applications in this book. They aren't often used to edit and enhance photographs and that's an integral part of digital scrapbooking.

Desktop publishing programs, such as Microsoft Publisher, are excellent choices for page layouts because they're designed for print. If you plan to use your digital layouts as image files only, this type of application wouldn't be a good choice. They also lack robust editing and image creation tools, so you'll likely still want a good paint program to work with your photos and create embellishments.

Some page layout programs are integrated with other application types by the same software manufacturer. For example, Adobe's Photoshop, Illustrator, and InDesign use file types that are compatible and can be exported quickly from one application to another. This suite of applications is expensive, but if this type of package interests you, you might want to look at Serif's PhotoPlus, DrawPlus, and PagePlus applications. They're integrated as well and reasonably priced. In this book, we'll use PhotoPlus for some of our examples.

Software Used in This Book

Since we'll concentrate on paint applications in this book, you can expect to see examples created in various image editors. We'll use the following applications throughout this book:

- Adobe Photoshop Elements 2.0
- Jasc Paint Shop Pro 8.1
- Microsoft Digital Image Pro 9
- Serif PhotoPlus 9
- Ulead PhotoImpact XL

All of these applications can be purchased at local stores, online at various resellers, and at the manufacturer's site. Please check this book's Appendix A for Web site addresses.

And Away We Go!

Time to start scrapbooking. Haul out those photos, and let's start creating some memories (see Figure 1.14).

Figure 1.14 "Butterfly" by Margie Lundy.

2

Digital Photo Fundamentals

I n this chapter, we'll look at some digital photo essentials, including camera and scanning tips and basic photo correction. For many scrappers, the topics covered in Chapter 2 are all you'll need to know to improve the photos in your scrapbooks. For folks who'd like to go beyond the basics, we'll look at more sophisticated photo enhancing methods in Chapter 7, "Advanced Photo Techniques."

Digital Camera Basics

These days digital cameras are so affordable that they are within easy reach of almost any computer user. In fact, many computer manufacturers bundle digital cameras with their entry-level home computers. The quality of the photos you get will depend on your camera. Some of the bundled cameras might be fine for producing photos for display on Web pages, but not quite what you'd want for anything but the smallest of print images. Let's review some of the basics of digital cameras to be sure that the camera you use is right for the job.

Resolution: Megapixels and You

If you know nothing else about digital cameras, you probably know that *megapixels* (MP) have something to do with the quality of the photos a digital camera produces. What are megapixels and why are they important?

Pixels are the basic blocks of color that make up a digital image, and megapixels are the millions of pixels that a camera can capture. The megapixel count of a photo is usually referred to as the photo's *resolution*, and resolution is one of the major factors determining the quality of the photo and how it can be used. Other factors include the type of light sensors used in your camera and the amount and kind of compression, if any, that your camera applies to captured images.

Early digital cameras had resolutions of only 1 MP or 2 MP. Many of today's cameras have resolutions of 6 MP or more. For printed photos and scrapbook pages, you'll want a camera with a resolution of at least 3 MP, which is fine for 8 × 10 inch photo prints and pages up to 12 × 12 inch.

Focus

All digital cameras include automatic focus. This suits most purposes, although sometimes you'll want to have more control over what areas of your photo are in sharp focus and what areas are not. For example, you may be shooting a photo of a person who happens to be standing several feet in front of a building that occupies the center of your composition. In this case, you want to be sure that it's the person and not the building that's in focus. Since the automatic focus targets the center of your photo, you'd have a problem here. You can avoid this problem by using your camera's manual focus control, if there is one.

TIP

There is a way around the person-in-front-of-the-building problem even if you have only automatic focus. Nearly all digital cameras let you lock the focus by pressing the shutter release button only halfway down, not actually taking the photo until you press the button all the way down. So, what you can do is center the focus target over the thing you want in focus, press the shutter release button halfway down and hold it, compose your photo as you like, and then press the shutter release all the way down.

Exposure

Cameras produce photos by capturing light. The amount of light that enters the camera is the *exposure*. By controlling the exposure, you control which areas of the photo show detail, whether areas of motion are frozen or blurred, and how much of the photo is in sharp focus.

If you let in too little light, your photo will be underexposed, making the image overly dark and obscuring detail in the shadow areas. If you let in too much light, your photo will be overexposed, washing out the image's colors and eliminating detail in the highlight areas.

Two things control exposure: shutter speed and aperture. Shutter speed controls how long a time light is allowed to enter the camera. Aperture controls how large the opening is that lets in the light. Longer shutter speeds blur areas of motion, while shorter shutter speeds freeze areas of motion. Larger apertures reduce the area of sharp focus, while smaller apertures increase the area of sharp focus.

NOTE

Aperture is measured in f-numbers. The larger the f-number, the smaller the aperture. Shutter speed is measured in fractions of seconds and seconds.

All digital cameras have automatic exposure controls, and in many cases that's sufficient. If you want to have more control over exposure, you'll want a camera with semi-automatic exposure controls or even manual exposure controls. Here are the possibilities:

- **Fully automatic.** The camera determines both the shutter speed and aperture.
- **Aperture priority.** You set the aperture and the camera chooses an appropriate shutter speed. This allows you to control *depth of field*, the areas of sharp focus.
- **Shutter priority.** You set the shutter speed and the camera chooses an appropriate aperture. This allows you to freeze motion or allow blurring of areas of motion.
- **Manual.** You control both the aperture and shutter speed.

Lenses

Early digital cameras had only unremovable fixed-focus lenses, which were fine for snapshots of landscapes and group portraits, but not so good for portraits of individuals or for close close-ups. Nearly all digital cameras today come with zoom lenses, enabling you to change the focal length of the lens as suits the situation, from wide-angle to telephoto. Table 2.1 summarizes uses of typical focal lengths for built-in digital camera lenses.

Table 2.1 Typical focal lengths and their uses

Focal Length	Lens Type	Typical Uses
4.5mm	Wide-angle	Landscapes and group portraits
6.5mm	Wide-angle	Landscapes and building interiors
10mm	Normal	Approximates what the human eye sees
19mm	Telephoto	Portraits
37mm	Telephoto	Frame-filling shots of distant objects and wildlife

NOTE

Some digital cameras have lens converters for ultra wide-angle or long telephoto. Some have a macro or close-focus feature that lets you take very close close-ups.

If your digital camera budget is unlimited, you can even consider a digital SLR, which has a camera body much like a 35mm film camera and removable lenses (some lenses being identical to those used with film cameras). These cameras produce high-quality photos, but the prices are steep.

WARNING

When looking for a digital camera with a zoom lens, pay attention only to the optical zoom capabilities. Totally ignore any claims about digital zoom because you should never use digital zoom.

Optical zoom controls real physical magnification. Digital zoom simply resizes and crops the captured image, reducing image quality along the way.

Memory and Power Sources

Although your digital camera doesn't use any film, it does need a place to store images. There are several kinds of storage for digital cameras, and different brands and models of cameras use different kinds of storage. Some common storage media types are Compact Flash cards, SmartMedia cards, Memory Sticks, and the new (and tiny) xD-Picture Cards. Be sure to get the right kind of memory media for your camera—and plenty of it. You don't want to run out of storage space far from your computer right in the middle of an important event that you'd like to record.

You'll also need batteries for your camera. Use rechargeables if you can, and keep some spare batteries on hand. You don't want to have your batteries die just as you're about to take an important shot.

TIP

To prolong their life, rechargeable NiCad and NiMH batteries need to be fully dis-
charged before recharging. Get a charger that includes a discharge function, and discharge your batteries before charging them again. (RadioShack carries chargers with
a discharge function, and you can probably find them at many other sources as well,
such as your local camera shop or online photo supply store.)

In addition to batteries, you'll probably want an AC adapter for your camera. You can
use the adapter when you're offloading your photos to your computer. That way, you'll
save your batteries for when you really need them. You can also use the adapter as your
power source for indoor shots such as portraits or still lifes.

Other Considerations

This information just touches on what's involved in digital photography. Be sure to
check your camera's documentation for other topics such as white balance, different
types of metering, and any special features that are available on your camera. If you
don't yet have a camera, check out the Web sites of different manufacturers, such as
Canon, Epson, Fujifilm, HP, Kodak, Minolta, Nikon, Olympus, Pentax, and Sony. Also,
take a look at the reviews and useful content at Digital Photography Review
(www.dpreview.com).

TIP

When shopping for a digital camera, there are two things that you might overlook
but are important: fit and ease-of-use. What is the weight and balance of the camera? How does it feel in your hand? Are the controls readily accessible, and are they
intuitive? The fanciest state-of-the-art camera is of no value if it isn't fun to use, so be
sure that you and your camera are compatible.

Scanning Basics

If your photos are ones you've taken with a digital camera, then it's a simple matter to
save your photos to your computer using either the camera's software, the operating
system's media support, or image editing software. However, if you have physical photo
prints or slides, you'll need to scan your photos in order to get digital versions.

Most copying services can scan your photos for you. You can also scan the photos yourself using a desktop flatbed scanner (see Figure 2.1).

Figure 2.1 You can scan your film photos at home with a flatbed scanner.

There are quite a few good personal scanners available from manufacturers such as Epson and HP. For photo scanning, you'll want one with an optical resolution of at least 600 dots per inch (dpi)—1,200 dpi or 2,400 dpi preferred—and at least 24-bit color depth. If you want to scan slides or negatives, be sure the scanner includes a transparency adapter. At the time of writing this book, a good 2,400 dpi scanner with transparency adapter can be purchased for as little as US$150.

Resolution

One of the most basic, but sometimes confusing, scanning topics is resolution. When speaking of scanning, resolution doesn't refer to the total number of pixels or megapixels like digital camera resolution. Instead, scanner resolution refers to the number of samples per inch or dots per inch that the scanner reads.

The easiest way to approach scanner resolution is to look at a real example. Suppose you have an 8 × 10 inch photo that you want to scan. If you scan this photo at 200 dpi (that is, 200 dots per inch), you'll get a digital image that's 200 dpi × 8 inches by 200 dpi × 10 inches—1,600 pixels by 2,000 pixels. (Each dot or sample scanned yields one pixel in your digital image.) If you scanned the same image at 400 dpi, you'd get an image that's 400 dpi × 8 inches by 400 dpi × 10 inches—3,200 pixels by 4000 pixels. If you were to save each of these scans at 200 pixels per inch (ppi) and print each one at 100%, with no printer scaling, you'd get an 8 × 10 inch print in the first case and a 16 × 20 inch print in the second case.

NOTE

In the example, the 400 dpi scan would take up four times as much space on your hard drive as the 200 dpi scan because the 400 dpi version is both twice as high and twice as wide as the 200 dpi version.

A Few Tips

When you scan your photos, follow these bits of advice:

- Choose the settings appropriate for what you're scanning. Prints should be scanned using your scanner's full color or grayscale settings (full color for color photos and either full color or grayscale for black and white). Negatives and slides should be scanned with transparency settings, if available, and you may also need to tell your scanner whether the transparency you're scanning is a negative.

- Choose the appropriate resolution. If you'll print your photos at an image resolution of 200 ppi, then scan at 200 dpi to get a print that's the same size as the physical photo. If you want to print at a larger size than the original, increase the scan resolution in order to get a larger number of pixels. For example, to print a 4×5 inch original at 8×10 inch with an image resolution of 200 ppi, set the scan resolution to 400 dpi. Your scanned image will then be 1,600 pixels – 2,000 pixels, just what you need for an 8×10 inch print of a 200 ppi image.

- If you're interested in only a part of the original, scan only that part. Virtually all scanners have a means of restricting the scan to a portion of the original. You'll probably want that smaller portion to print at larger than its original size, so remember to increase the scan resolution to get all the pixels you need to make a larger print.

For a lot more information on scanning, head over to Wayne Fulton's Scan Tips at www.scantips.com.

TIP

You can scan 3D objects as well as photos on your scanner. Buttons, door keys, and other objects can be scanned to use as scrapbook elements in your digital layouts. Just lift up the scanner cover or remove it completely, place the objects on the scanner bed, drape a cloth over the objects to cover the scanner bed, and then scan as you normally would.

Rotating and Straightening

Many times you'll find that the photos you scan or offload from your digital camera aren't quite straight or maybe they're in landscape orientation when you really want portrait orientation. All image editors (and most photo album applications) provide tools for rotating and straightening your images.

Rotating

The photo in Figure 2.2 is an example where the photo is in landscape instead of portrait.

Getting images like this into an upright position is easy—you just need to rotate them 90°. Some image editors have special commands just for cases like this:

Figure 2.2 A photo that needs its orientation adjusted.

Paint Shop Pro 8.1

> Image > Rotate > Clockwise 90

> Image > Rotate > Counter-clockwise 90

PhotoImpact XL

> Edit > Rotate & Flip > Rotate Left 90°

> Edit > Rotate & Flip > Rotate Right 90°

Photoshop Elements 2.0

> Image > Rotate > 90° Left

> Image > Rotate > 90° Right

There are other, more general ways to get the orientation right as well and all image editors include one or more means of freely rotating an image:

Digital Image Pro 9

> Format > Rotate > Canvas

Paint Shop Pro 8.1

> Image > Rotate > Free Rotate

> Deform tool

PhotoImpact XL

> Transform tool

PhotoPlus 9

> Image > Rotate
>
> Deform tool

Photoshop Elements 2.0

> Image > Rotate > Custom
>
> Image > Transform > Free Transform

Commands for freely rotating an image usually include settings for rotating 90° clockwise (right) or counterclockwise (left), 180°, and maybe 270°. In addition, free rotation commands have a control that lets you enter other values, enabling you to tilt your image any way you like.

Deform or Transform tools also enable you to rotate an image in any way. When such a tool is active, you can drag with the mouse to rotate your image. (See your application's documentation for precise instructions.) Figure 2.3 shows an image being freely rotated in PhotoPlus 9, using the Deform tool.

Figure 2.3 Images can be freely rotated using an image editor's Deform or Transform tool.

NOTE

Your image editor might also include commands for changing the original photo to its mirror image or for flipping the photo horizontally or vertically.

Straightening

Figure 2.4 shows an example photo where the camera wasn't held level when the photo was taken.

It's quite easy to fix photos that weren't level when shot or scanned photos where the photo wasn't lying straight on the scanner bed during the scan. Your first impulse might be to use your application's free rotate command or Deform/Transform tool to get the angle right. That would work, but it usually requires quite a lot of care and guesswork.

Figure 2.4 A photo that needs to be straightened.

A far more easy solution is to use your image editor's dedicated straightening command or tool:

Digital Image Pro 9

> Format > Straighten Picture > Canvas

Paint Shop Pro 8.1

> Straighten tool

PhotoImpact XL

> Transform tool

PhotoPlus 9

> Image > Rotate

Photoshop Elements 2.0

> Image > Rotate > Straighten

Figure 2.5 shows the example image from Figure 2.4 being straightened with PhotoImpact's Transform tool with the Rotate method set to Rotate using a horizontal line. Figure 2.6 shows the straightened result after cropping.

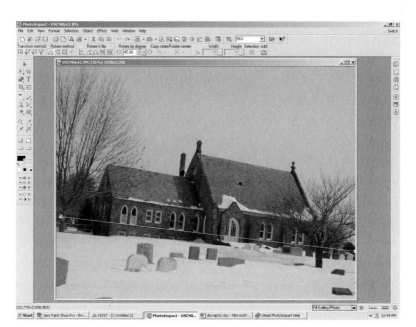

Figure 2.5 Straightening the photo.

Figure 2.6 The straightened result.

Quick Fixes

Getting your photo straight or in the proper orientation is only the first step. Almost all digital photos need some adjustment to their color and contrast. In addition to including commands for photographers who want to have full control over these sorts of adjustments, most image editors also include automatic photo correction tools that anyone can use with ease.

If you don't know a lot about digital photography—or sometimes even if you do—you'll find your image editor's automatic photo correction tools quite useful. Some editors provide the means for a really quick fix. For example, Paint Shop Pro users can try zapping their photos with OneStepPhotoFix, available on the Photo toolbar or the Script palette. Although a quick fix will sometimes give unacceptable results, in most cases, your photo is improved. For example, notice the improvement in color and contrast shown in Figure 2.7, where OneStepPhotoFix is applied to a photo straight from the camera. The original version appears on the left, with the fixed version on the right.

For a little more control, try using individual correction commands one by one. In most cases, this sequence of command types yields the best result:

1. Color balance
2. Contrast enhancement
3. Saturation enhancement

Figure 2.7 Many photos can benefit from your image editor's quick-fix tools.

Color balance corrects the color of your photo. Contrast enhancement corrects contrast (the difference between dark tones and light tones), providing your photo with more definition. After correcting the contrast, you'll usually find that the colors are washed out. Saturation enhancement can put some verve back into those colors.

The reason you'd want to use the separate commands, rather than your image editor's automatic correction command, is so you can tweak the settings to best suit the specific photo. For example, you might want to increase or decrease the strength of the contrast adjustment. Or, if your photo is a portrait, you'll want to make sure the saturation enhancement doesn't increase the saturation to unnatural levels.

Here's a list of quick-fix photo improvement commands available in some of the most popular image editors, including one-step fixes and commands that allow tweaking:

Digital Image Pro 9

   Touchup > Contrast Auto Fix

   Touchup > Levels Auto Fix

   Touchup > Adjust Tint

Paint Shop Pro 8.1

   OneStepPhotoFix script

   Adjust > Color Balance > Automatic Color Balance

   Adjust > Brightness and Contrast > Automatic Contrast Enhancement

   Adjust > Brightness and Contrast > Clarify

   Adjust > Hue and Saturation > Automatic Saturation Enhancement

PhotoImpact XL

> Effect > Photographic > Express Fix
>
> Format > Auto-process > Level
>
> Format > Auto-process > Adjust
>
> Format > Auto-process > Color
>
> Format > Auto-process > Enhance
>
> Format > Auto-process > Contrast

PhotoPlus 9

> Image > Adjust > Auto Levels
>
> Image > Adjust > Auto Contrast

Photoshop Elements 2.0

> Enhance > Quick Fix
>
> Enhance > Auto Levels
>
> Enhance > Auto Contrast
>
> Enhance > Auto Color Correction

Noise Reduction

Digital photos can include quite a bit of *noise*—random dots of color scattered throughout the image. This is particularly common in photos that are somewhat under-exposed or contain large areas of blue. Figure 2.8 shows a photo that exhibits a good deal of noise.

Figure 2.8 Digital photos can be marred by noise.

Image editors provide one or more commands for reducing noise and other specks, such as dust spots on scanned images:

Digital Image Pro 9

> Touchup > Remove Spots or Blemishes

Paint Shop Pro 8.1

> Adjust > Add/Remove Noise > Edge Preserving Smooth
>
> Adjust > Add/Remove Noise > Despeckle
>
> Adjust > Add/Remove Noise > Median
>
> Adjust > Add/Remove Noise > Salt and Pepper Filter

PhotoImpact XL

> Effect > Noise > Despeckle

PhotoPlus 9

> Effects > Noise > Median

Photoshop Elements 2.0

> Filter > Noise > Despeckle
>
> Filter > Noise > Median

Each of these methods works by blurring small areas that contrast with surrounding areas so that those areas of high contrast blend into the surrounding areas. Some noise reduction commands, like Paint Shop Pro's Edge Preserving Smooth, try to maintain edges while blurring more random areas of contrast. Some, like Median, affect the whole image, edges and all. Whenever you use a noise reduction command, try to use the smallest setting you can so that you don't also lose real image details along with the noise.

Blurring and Sharpening

Differences in focus can create differences in mood in your photos. Subjects in sharp focus grab your attention, and subjects in soft focus seem dreamy or romantic. The amount of focus for the parts of the photo other than the subject (that is, the depth of field) also affects the feel of your photo. For example, compare the photos in Figures 2.9 and 2.10, where the photo on the left shows both the subject and the background in sharp focus and the photo on the right shows the subject in focus, but the background is blurred.

Figure 2.9 Broad depth of field keeps everything in focus.

Figure 2.10 Shallow depth of field blurs areas that are away from the subject.

If your camera has controls for aperture or specialized controls for different sorts of scenes, you can control the depth of field when you take your picture. You can also modify the sharpness of your photo (or parts of your photo) using the blurring and sharpening tools and commands available in your image editor.

Gaussian Blur

Most image editors have several blurring commands in addition to noise reduction commands, which also produce blurring. The one blurring command that's most useful for photos is Gaussian Blur. With Gaussian Blur, you can simulate shallow depth of field by selecting the foreground and the background and blurring them, leaving the subject sharp. Compare the photo in Figure 2.11, where the subject, the foreground, and the background are all sharp, with the version in Figure 2.12, where the foreground and background are blurred with Gaussian Blur.

Figure 2.11 Photo with the foreground, background, and subject all in focus.

Figure 2.12 Simulated shallow depth of field using Gaussian Blur.

You control the amount of blurring with Gaussian Blur's single control labeled "Radius" or "Amount," depending on which image editor you're using. (In the case of Digital Image Pro, there's no label at all.) Figure 2.13 shows the dialog box for Gaussian Blur in PhotoPlus 9.

Figure 2.13 Gaussian Blur's single control determines the amount of blurring.

TIP

> In photos with a shallow depth of field, areas in front of the subject as well as areas behind the subject are blurred. Areas that are closer to the subject—whether in front of the subject or behind—are less blurred than areas farther from the subject. Therefore, to get the most realistic simulation of shallow depth of field, apply different amounts of blurring to different areas of your photo, with most blurring in the areas farthest from the subject.

Here's where you'll find Gaussian Blur in some popular image editors:

Digital Image Pro 9

Touchup > Gaussian Blur

Paint Shop Pro 8.1

Adjust > Blur > Gaussian Blur

PhotoImpact XL

> Effect > Blur > Gaussian Blur

PhotoPlus 9

> Effects > Blur > Gaussian Blur

Photoshop Elements 2.0

> Filter > Blur > Gaussian Blur

NOTE

Your image editor might also include a command for Soft Focus, which produces a dreamy scattered light effect in addition to blurring.

Unsharp Mask

Image editors usually include several sharpening commands, but by far the best for photo work is Unsharp Mask. You use Unsharp Mask to give a little more definition to digital photos (which tend to be less sharp than film photos) and to restore sharpness to photos to which you've applied noise reduction. Figure 2.14 shows the Unsharp Mask dialog box in PhotoPlus 9.

Figure 2.14 Sharpening a photo with Unsharp Mask.

Unsharp Mask has three controls:

- **Amount.** This setting affects contrast. For grainy images, use a low setting (15–20). For other photos, you can have a setting as high as 200. Increase the setting until the sharpening is a bit too strong, and then turn it back down gradually until the sharpening looks rather good. If you see obvious halos along areas of contrast, the setting is too high. (This control is called Contrast in Digital Image Pro and Strength in Paint Shop Pro.)

- **Radius.** With high values for Amount, use a low Radius (0.5–1.5). With low Amount values, you'll need higher Radius settings (5 or more). Typically, you'll get good results with Amount set to 100–150 and Radius set to 0.5–1.5. (This control is called Edge Width in Digital Image Pro.)

■ **Threshold**. Threshold determines how different two areas need to be before sharpening takes place. When Threshold is set to 0, everything is sharpened. The higher the value for Threshold, the more different two areas must be before sharpening kicks in. For portraits and other photos where areas of smoothness are important, you'll need a relatively high setting for Threshold. In general, it's best to start at 0 and gradually increase the Threshold until you get the result you want. (This control is called Noise Reduction Threshold in Digital Image Pro and Clipping in Paint Shop Pro.)

TIP

Images that you intend to display on a video monitor should be sharpened so that they appear appropriately sharp when you view them in your image editor. Images that you intend to print should look slightly oversharpened on your monitor.

Here's where to find Unsharp Mask in some popular image editors:

Digital Image Pro 9

Touchup > Unsharp Mask

Paint Shop Pro 8.1

Adjust > Sharpness > Unsharp Mask

PhotoImpact XL

Effect > Sharpen > Unsharp Mask

PhotoPlus 9

Effects > Sharpen > Unsharp Mask

Photoshop Elements 2.0

Filter > Sharpen > Unsharp Mask

NOTE

Unsharp Mask's name might seem rather confusing, because you want to sharpen your image, not make it unsharp. This seemingly odd name comes from the process's origins in the physical darkroom, where a blurred version of a negative was used to create sharpening.

Photo Enhancement

Some digital photos need more than color correction, noise reduction, or sharpening. These might be scans of old photos that have been physically damaged, photos that include extraneous elements that you'd like to remove, or portraits that feature those creepy glowing irises known as *red eye*. Now we'll take a look at how to correct these types of problems.

Repairing Scratches

Old photos are sometimes marred by scratches, and scans of even pristine photos might sometimes suffer from an inadvertent hair lying on the scanner bed. Scratch removal tools can come to the rescue in these cases and can also be used to remove facial blemishes in portraits.

Here are some tools and commands that are handy for repairing scratches:

Digital Image Pro 9

Touchup > Blending Brush

Paint Shop Pro 8.1

Adjust > Add/Remove Noise > Automatic Small Scratch Removal

Scratch Remover tool

PhotoImpact XL

Clone brush tools

PhotoPlus 9

Effects > Noise > Dust and Scratch Remover

Photoshop Elements 2.0

Filter > Noise > Dust & Scratches

The scratch removing commands work by analyzing your photo and then blurring the parts that the command interprets as a scratch. Scratch removing tools work similarly, except that you control where the scratch removal is applied by dragging the tool along the scratch.

TIP

When using a scratch remover tool, make a series of short drags rather than one long continuous drag. That way, you'll have much more control and the result will look more natural.

Cloning

Cloning is taking image data from one section of an image and copying that data onto another area of the image. All image editors have some kind of cloning tool:

Digital Image Pro 9
>   Touchup > Clone Brush

Paint Shop Pro 8.1
>   Clone brush

PhotoImpact XL
>   Clone brush tools

PhotoPlus 9
>   Clone tool

Photoshop Elements 2.0
>   Clone Stamp tool

One of the handiest uses for cloning tools is to correct blemishes in a photo. Set the source point for the copying by right-clicking, Shift-clicking, or clicking (depending on which application you're using), and then paint to cover the blemish by dragging with the left mouse button down. For best results, use short strokes or dabs rather than long strokes. Figure 2.15 shows a photo in need of cloning, and Figure 2.16 shows some cloning in progress in Digital Image Pro 9.

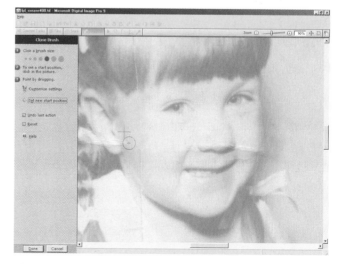

Figure 2.15 A damaged photo in need of cloning.

Figure 2.16 Creases and splotches can be eliminated with cloning.

For best results, use a soft edge for your clone brush and adjust the size as needed. Don't hesitate to change the source point or brush size as you go.

You might also get better results if you reduce the opacity of your brush so that the cloned image data is semi-transparent. That way, you can dab multiple times to build up the effect until you get just what you want. This is an especially good idea when you're working on areas of a person's face, where a delicate touch is key.

TIP

Besides using clone tools to repair damage to photos such as cracks, tears, and creases, you can also use clone tools to cover up a mole on a person's face. You can even remove large areas of a photo, such as electrical wires or your cousin's former spouse.

Dodging and Burning

Dodge and Burn tools can be used to lighten overly dark areas (Dodge) or darken overly light areas (Burn). Typically, these tools are like paintbrushes, but instead of applying paint, these brushes modify the pixels that are already present in your digital image.

To use these tools, set the brush size as you would any other brush tool in your image editor. Set the edge of the brush so that it's rather soft and set the strength of the effect quite low. In some image editors, the setting to use for reducing the strength is labeled "Opacity," and settings of 10 (or even less) will probably yield the best results.

Paint over the areas that you want to change. Short strokes or dabs are usually best. If you make a mistake, use your image editor's Undo feature to undo the last stroke, and then reapply.

In most image editors, the Dodge and Burn tools are available on the palette that holds tools. In Digital Image Pro, Dodge and Burn are accessed with Touchup > Other Photo Repair > Dodge and Burn Brush.

NOTE

Your image editor may have other photo retouching tools in addition to tools for dodging and burning. These might include brushes for localized blurring or sharpening, brushes for localized adjustments to color and saturation, and brushes for smudging areas of the image together.

Red Eye Reduction

You've probably seen it a lot: those shiny demonic-looking red or greenish pupils that mar portraits of your family, friends, and pets. Don't despair—red eye is something that's easy to fix.

Image editors take two approaches to fixing red eye. One is to use a brush tool. In this case, you select the color that you want to change and the new color that you want to use, set the brush size, and dab on the red eye area. The other approach is to have a command that pops up a dialog box where you can select the areas to change, and then adjust settings to get just the right effect. Figure 2.17 shows Paint Shop Pro's Red-eye Removal in action.

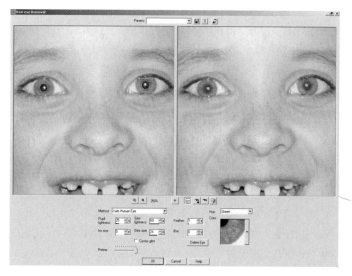

Figure 2.17 Eliminating red eye.

Here's where to find the red-eye reduction tool or command in some popular image editors:

Digital Image Pro 9

Touchup > Fix Red Eye

Paint Shop Pro 8.1

Adjust > Red-eye Removal

PhotoImpact XL

Effect > Photographic > Remove Red Eye

PhotoPlus 9

Effects > Other > Fix Red Eye

Photoshop Elements 2.0

Red Eye Brush tool

Although it's not difficult to get rid of red eye, it's even handier to avoid it altogether. Red eye typically occurs when the light of your camera's flash reflects off the retinas of your subject. One way to avoid red eye is simply to not use your flash, but of course, that's not always feasible. Here are a couple other workarounds:

- If your camera has a pre-flash or red-eye reduction feature, give it a try. The short burst of light before the actual flash causes your subject's pupils to constrict, reducing the amount of light reaching the subject's retinas. However, keep in mind that some folks might find the pre-flash annoying.

- Use a flash attachment that can be held at a different angle than the head-on angle of the camera lens. This way, the light from the flash won't be directed right into your subject's eyes and reflected back to the camera.

Cropping and Resizing

For a finishing touch, you may want to change the size of your photo. There are two ways to change an image's size: cropping and resizing. Cropping cuts away some of the original photo. You lose some of the data, but the quality of the image doesn't change. Resizing keeps all of the areas that appeared in the original photo, but quality can be noticeably degraded.

Cropping

Cropping is used primarily to improve the composition of a photo. For example, take the photo shown in Figure 2.18. The little boy is obviously the intended subject here, but he's lost in the surrounding space.

Figure 2.18 A photo in need of cropping.

Now take a look at the cropped version in Figure 2.19. Here the observer's attention is clearly directed to the boy—a much more interesting composition.

Here's a list of the major cropping tools in popular image editors (and some editors include a few other means of cropping as well):

Digital Image Pro 9

> Format > Crop > Canvas

Paint Shop Pro 8.1

> Crop Tool

PhotoImpact XL

> Format > Auto-process > Crop
>
> Crop tool

PhotoPlus 9

> Crop tool

Photoshop Elements 2.0

> Image > Crop
>
> Crop tool

Figure 2.19 Cropping directs attention to the subject, creating a more interesting image.

Resizing

When you resize an image, you don't cut any of the image away. Instead, you stretch the image out to make it larger or squash it down to make it smaller. When you increase an image's size, the image editor does an *interpolation*, making its best guess at what the added pixels should look like and then sticking those new pixels in amid the existing pixels. When you decrease an image's size, the image editor chooses pixels to throw away or combine.

Keep in mind that you'll get the best results if you maintain the original image's *aspect ratio* (its ratio of height to width). Also, you'll almost always get better results when decreasing the image's size than when increasing the size.

TIP

Reducing an image's size can produce blurring. You'll almost always want to sharpen your image a bit after reducing its size.

Figure 2.20 shows the Resize dialog box in Photoshop Elements 2.0. The following is a list of resizing commands in popular image editors:

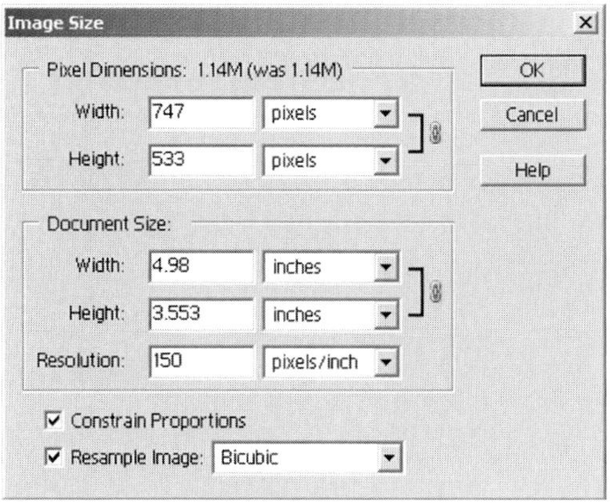

Digital Image Pro 9

> Format > Resize Image

Paint Shop Pro 8.1

> Image > Resize

PhotoImpact XL

> Format > Image Size

PhotoPlus 9

> Image > Image Size

Photoshop Elements 2.0

> Image > Resize > Image Size

Figure 2.20 Resizing an image.

Most image editors let you change the image size in terms of either pixels, percentages, or print size (usually in inches or centimeters and possibly other units). In nearly all cases, the Resize dialog box also gives you the option of changing the image resolution (the number of pixels per inch) either in conjunction with resizing or without any change in your image's dimensions. To change the resolution without changing the dimensions, be sure to deselect whatever control in your image editor triggers resampling. (We'll look more closely at print size and image resolution in Chapter 8, "Sharing Your Work.")You'll have the option of constraining your image's proportions (aspect ratio). In order to prevent distortion, you'll want to be sure that this option is selected. You'll also have a variety of resizing methods from which to choose. These include things like *Bicubic* and *Bilinear*. Bicubic is usually the best option to choose when you want to increase the size of your image. Bicubic might also work well when decreasing the image's size, but if the results are too blurry, try Bilinear instead. Paint Shop Pro also includes a resampling method option called Smart Resize, which analyzes your image and chooses the best resampling method for that image.

TIP

> You can also resize an image or layer with your editor's Deform or Transform tool, if available. Do any resizing and rotating with a Deform/Transform tool all at once in order to avoid image degradation. In other words, choose the tool and do all your resizing and rotating before selecting another tool.

A Few Last Words

Before leaving this chapter, here's one more important tip. Whenever you edit a digital photo or scan, edit a copy rather than the original. Keep the original as is and store it away for safe keeping. That way, you can always go back if you want to make a new attempt at editing the photo. For example, it's possible to make a mistake from which it's hard to recover, or at sometime in the future you may learn a new editing technique that can produce better results than current techniques, or your image editing skills might improve. In cases like this, you'll be happy to have a copy of the original photo on hand.

And one last "last word" on basic photo editing: never work on a JPEG version of your image. JPEG uses a form of compression that throws away bits of your image. The image quality is diminished each time you edit a JPEG image, save it to disk, and close the image. To avoid this, save your edited photo in a format that uses no compression or that uses a type of compression that doesn't throw away image data. Appropriate formats include TIFF, PNG, and the native format of your image editor, such as Paint Shop Pro's PspImage format or Photoshop Element's PSD format.

AMERICAN MADE · CAN MADE · AMERICAN · ERICAN MADE · AMERICAN M · AMERIC · U.S.A · USA · MARGIE

3

Basic Layout Guidelines

In this chapter, you'll learn the basics of page design and how to set up scrapbook pages in a number of popular applications. Color schemes and design will also be discussed.

Last Things First: Is That Your Final Output?

It might seem a little odd to worry about the final stage of your layout first, but the way you intend to display it will determine how you make it. Traditionally, scrapbook pages are printed and placed in plastic sleeve protectors and then into albums. However, digital scrapbookers have other options to store and share their layouts. Page designs can be burned to CD or stored on other media for later printing, or perhaps never printed at all, but rather viewed on a computer monitor or television screen. They can also be sized for display in a Web gallery, personal Web site, or multimedia slide show, or sent as an e-mail attachment.

Determining how you want the final product to be produced is sometimes a matter of cost or storage space. It's also possible to produce a design for display in *all* the ways discussed—perhaps you'll want a printed album for yourself, a slide show on CD for relatives, and a Web gallery for friends near and far to view. This is one of the advantages to digital scrapbooking; you can do all the creative work once and produce multiple versions in a snap.

Once you have a good idea how you'll use the page design, the most important question to answer is what size to make it? If you plan to print the design you should have a specific album size in mind, whether it's 8.5 × 11 inch or 5 × 7 inch, but what if you want to send it via e-mail as well?

A good rule of thumb is to design for the largest size you might need, and downsize from that image. Unless you think you will *never* want to print a specific design, always design for printed output, and create any smaller images and Web graphics from the original print layout. In Figure 3.1, a 12 × 12 inch printable layout is resized to a Web graphic, sized at 600 × 600 pixels, suitable for e-mail or for posting in a Web picture gallery.

Figure 3.1 A print layout resized in Photoshop Elements.

That Pesky Resolution Question Revisited

Resolution is a concept that stumps and stymies a lot of people. We've discussed resolution as it relates to taking digital photographs and scanning film photos and memorabilia, but now let's look at resolution for print and Web images. *Print resolution* refers to the capability of the printer in use to produce a finely-detailed image. A printer capable of high resolution will produce a better quality image than a low-resolution printer.

Print resolution is referred to in dots per inch, or dpi, and this is a measurement of the size of ink drops that the printer will apply to paper. It's possible to set different print resolutions for inkjet printers, but it's a function of the printer software and not the application you use to produce a layout. The higher the dpi a printer is capable of, the better quality print possible from that printer.

Image resolution for Web images is a completely different animal from print resolution. (In this book, we'll most often refer to image resolution.) *Image resolution* is the term used to describe the pixels that make up a computer-generated image. All digital images are made up of pixels, and can be viewed on a computer monitor screen. The computer doesn't know inches or centimeters—it only knows pixels, and it doesn't even know how big those pixels are. A computer monitor displays a pixel based on its own settings. If an image is 800 pixels wide on one monitor, it's still 800 pixels wide on any other monitor, no matter how big it might look on the screen.

Here's the confusing part. We want to design a layout that prints out in inches or centimeters, which are physical terms of measurement, but we need to design it on a computer monitor that only reads pixels. Our objective is to produce a layout that will print out nicely, but also not tax the computer resources so much that we can't process images quickly. For this reason, all layouts in this book are produced at an image resolution of 200 pixels per inch, which produce an excellent quality print layout, while still creating reasonably small-sized image files to work on with the average home computer. All resources found on the accompanying CD-ROM are also created at 200 pixels per inch.

Faux Paper-Style or Not?

Digital scrapbook layouts tend to fall into one of two distinct styles. One of these styles is a "faux paper" look—digital elements are created that simulate actual paper scrapbook embellishments with a high degree of realism. The more realistic something looks the better. This style of layout usually uses textured backgrounds that look like real paper, often adding simulated fibers and tags, photo mattes, and other decorative elements. Margie Lundy created the layout in Figure 3.2.

Figure 3.2 "Paper-style" layout by Margie Lundy.

Another style well-suited to digital scrap-booking is reminiscent of commercial print images; this style is commonly referred to as "graphic-design" style (see Figure 3.3). An example of this style is your favorite commercial print advertisements. Layouts created in this fashion don't incorporate a lot of simulated textures, but focus on the photographs. Fonts play an important part in this style of layout—most of the deco-ration is different font styles and sizes. Word art, normally associated with Microsoft's Word application, is useful in creating large text banners and journal blocks.

Figure 3.3 "Art Is," a graphic design-style layout by Kristin Cronin-Barrow, runner-up in the Scrapping Idol challenge at www.digitalscrapbookplace.com.

No matter which style you prefer, begin creating the layout by determining the fin-ished size, and how to create that image in the application of your choice.

Common Layout Sizes

Layouts can be printed in just about any imaginable size. How you'll print and store them will often determine the size you design, so let's discuss print sizes now.

12 × 12

The most popular size for paper scrapbook albums is 12 × 12 inches, as shown in Figure 3.4. This size album is widely available at many different price points, often on sale at discount and craft stores. It's popular because a single page is large enough to allow for large photos, or many small ones. In addition, an open album produces a two-page spread, which can be used for panoramic photo displays or to create a theme.

The disadvantage to this size layout is that it can be difficult and expensive to print. Most inkjet printers for the home consumer will comfortably print 8.5 × 11 inches, sometimes border-free. It's possible to have these layouts printed professionally, but again, it can be an expensive proposition.

Figure 3.4 12 × 12 two-page layout created by Sally Beacham.

NOTE

Some canny and frugal digital scrappers have their 12 × 12 inch layouts printed on 11 × 17 inch paper as a color photocopy at discount office supply stores. When trimmed, this photocopy yields an 11 × 11 inch layout, which can then be matted on standard 12 × 12 inch scrapbook cardstock, and mounted in the album.

8.5 × 11

Another popular layout size, again a holdover from the paper scrapbook market, is 8.5 × 11 inches. Albums in that size are commonly available, and occasionally you can even find an album in landscape orientation, leaving more layout options. This layout size can often be printed on an inkjet printer and standard photocopiers. However, if the printer isn't capable of borderless (full-bleed) printing, you still may not get a true full-size layout. Any border can be trimmed and the layout can be mounted on 8.5 × 11 inch cardstock before placement in the album.

8 × 10

An 8 × 10 inch layout has a number of advantages. It can be printed on a home inkjet printer as well as photocopiers, but it can also be printed as an 8 × 10 photograph. Stores such as Wal-Mart have instant photo developing kiosks in their photo lab sections, so this size can be done quickly. The layout can also be printed at a regular photo lab or through an online photo developer such as Shutterfly or Ofoto. Having a layout printed as a photo tends to be a bit more expensive than printing at home, but is a good option if you don't have a photo-quality printer.

Templates and premade layouts designed for 8.5 × 11 are often flexible enough to be used at the 8 × 10 size as well and vice versa. The larger 12 × 12 inch templates usually don't resize as well.

8 × 8 and Variations

There are several variations on the 12 × 12 inch square theme; 8 × 8 inch and 6 × 6 inch layouts are common. The 8 inch square layout is popular because it's the largest square size that can be easily printed on standard 8.5 × 11 inch printer or photo paper with borders. You can easily find 8 × 8 and 6 × 6 albums at craft stores, specialized scrapbook stores, and other discount stores. The 6 × 6 inch size is especially good for albums commemorating an event, where you might choose to use one photo per page to highlight various activities or people at the event.

Creating Your Layout

Enough talk about what your layout *could* look like, let's actually create one! We'll take a look at creating a new layout image in several applications.

Most applications have a menu entry under the File menu to create a new image. Adobe Photoshop Elements 2.0 allows you to name the image, choose height and width in inches or other unit of measure, as well as define the image resolution, in pixels per inch or centimeters (see Figure 3.5). You also have a choice of background color for the initial image—White, Transparent, or Background Color. "Background" refers to the Background Color setting in the Tool palette for this application.

You can also choose from a number of predefined image layouts in the Preset Sizes drop-down list, accessed by clicking the arrow to the right of the list title. In Figure 3.6, you'll see an available preset image size for 8 × 10.

This setting has an automatic resolution setting of 300 pixels per inch, so if you choose that setting, you may want to choose a lower resolution for the image. Just type the resolution you want in the dialog box, and click OK. You've just started a new image in Photoshop Elements.

For Paint Shop Pro 8.1, the process is similar. Click File > New and a New Image dialog box will open (see Figure 3.7). You can set the height, width, resolution, and type of background. For digital scrapbooking, you will want a raster background primarily, in 24-bit color depth.

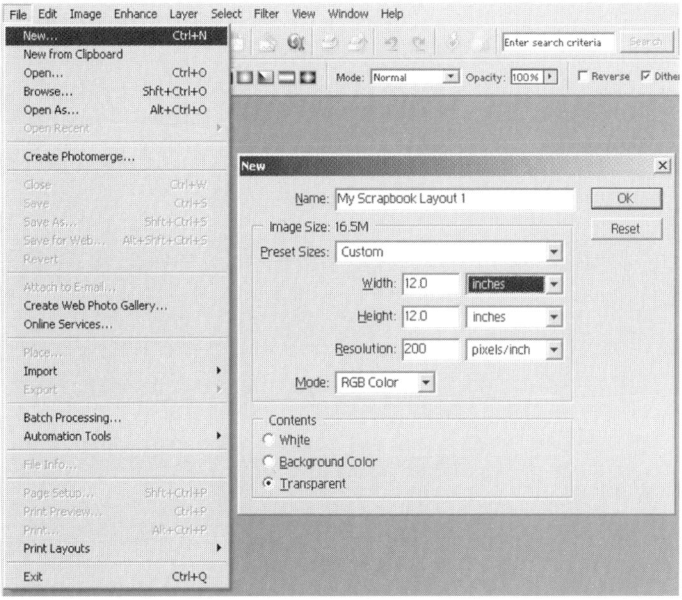

Figure 3.5 The New image dialog box in Adobe Photoshop Elements 2.0.

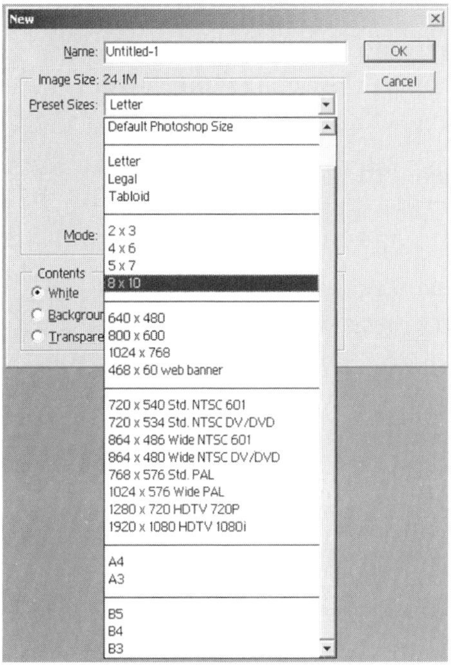

Figure 3.6 Preset image sizes available in Photoshop Elements 2.0.

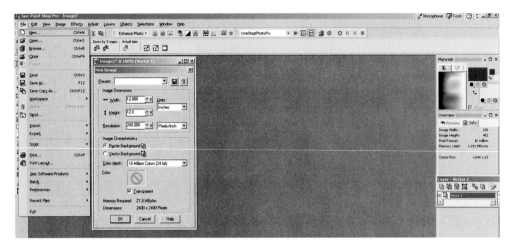

Figure 3.7 New image dialog box in Paint Shop Pro 8.1.

You can select either a Transparent background, or uncheck the Transparent check box and choose whatever color, pattern, or gradient that Paint Shop Pro 8.1 contains in its Materials Editor (see Figure 3.8). This dialog box allows you to choose a background color for the image as well as other colors for use in the application later.

In Microsoft's Digital Image Pro 9, the process is the same, but the interface looks quite a bit different. Click File > New and you'll see the New Image panel. Set the image height and width, or choose one of the preset sizes—there are 8 × 10 inch and "square" options. The square option sets the height and width at 7.5 inches. You can choose portrait or landscape orientations. To set the image resolution, you'll need to click the View advanced options button (see Figure 3.9). Click Done to create the new image.

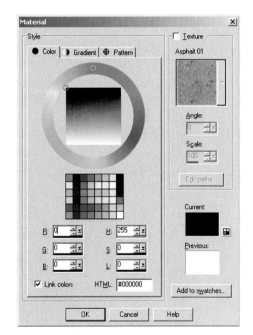

Figure 3.8 The Materials Editor in Paint Shop Pro 8.1.

Serif's PhotoPlus 9 has a simple New Image dialog box. Click File > New and enter the height and width in inches, centimeters, pixels or points, set the resolution, and choose the background—either White, Transparent, or the current image's Background Color (see Figure 3.10).

NOTE

Background color and *foreground color* are terms used in most paint programs to denote two separate color swatches that are active for use in the application. The terms are arbitrary and could just as easily be called "Color 1" and "Color 2" or "Bob" and "Fred." The terms exist to allow you to differentiate between the two color choices, and different tools and features may make use of one or both of these colors. In most of the New Image dialogs described thus far, the currently assigned Background Color is one of the image background options available when creating the new image.

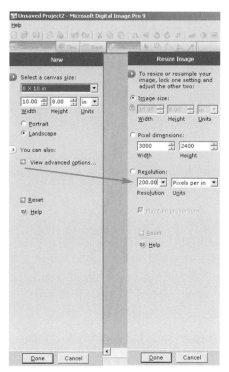

Figure 3.9 New Image panel in Microsoft Digital Image Pro 9.

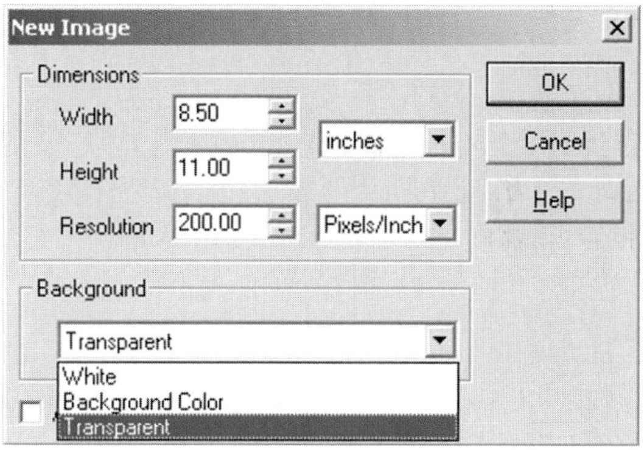

Figure 3.10 PhotoPlus 9's New Image dialog box.

PhotoImpact XL from Ulead gives you a great deal of flexibility when creating new images. Go to File > New > New Image and you can choose from Transparent, White, Background color, and Custom color canvas backgrounds (see Figure 3.11). The image resolution can be set from this dialog box as well as the color depth. You can also view the Preview pane to quickly check if the image size you've selected will be easily viewable with various output options (printed in portrait or landscape mode or various monitor screen resolutions).

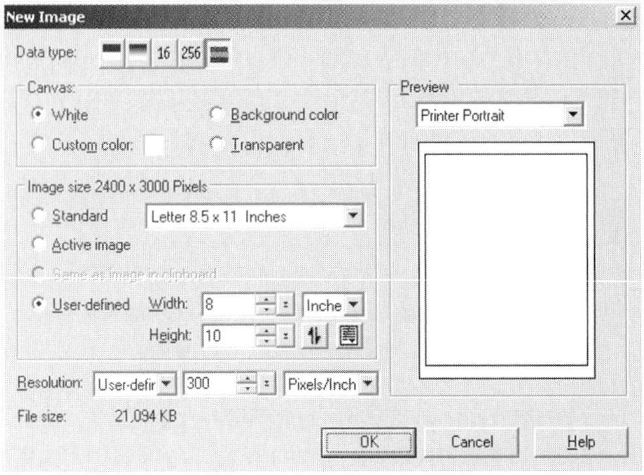

Figure 3.11 New Image dialog box in Ulead's PhotoImpact XL.

PhotoImpact's New Image dialog box also has a list of standard image sizes as well as user-defined custom sizes, which you can save to use quickly later (see Figure 3.12). The only caveat—the preset size doesn't retain the image resolution setting, so you'll have to set that manually each time if you usually change resolution settings for different images.

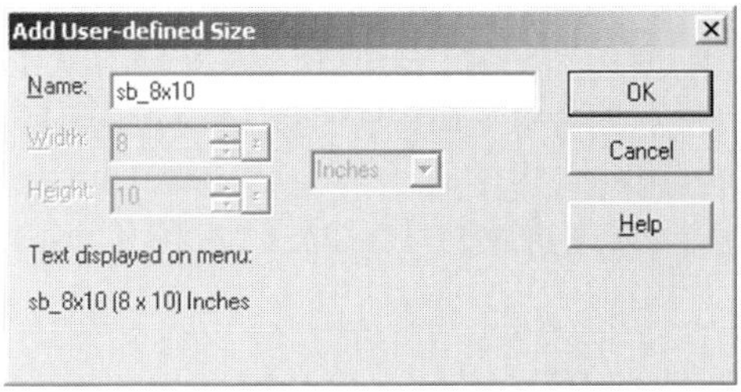

Figure 3.12 Adding a user-defined image size in PhotoImpact XL.

Now that you have an image open and ready for design, let's add some background color and pattern. Think of the background of your image as paper scrapbookers think of cardstock—the heavyweight paper that's used to mount other paper, photo, and objects, including memorabilia and embellishments. Of course, your digital background "paper" won't be any heavier in weight than any other image, but it will be the basic building component of the layout.

We've already chosen the photos with which we'd like to work, and now we need to determine a color scheme that will work to enhance, not overpower them. The photos are our memories, not the fancy scheme around them. So, let's always make sure the photos take center stage.

Color Options

Now's a good time to mention a few basics of color design. Color, as it applies to paper scrapbooking, is added to paper and embellishments by the manufacturer in the form of pigments, and is referred to as a *subtractive color model*. That is, the color you see is determined by the color of light reflected from the pigments on the page. If you have paper-scrapped in the past, you may have used a color wheel to help you choose colors that work well together. Colors are designated as:

- **Primary.** A "pure" color that can't be made by combining any other colors. Red, yellow, and blue are primary colors.
- **Secondary.** Colors that are made by combining primary colors—for example, orange, green, and violet.
- **Tertiary.** Colors that are made by combining a primary and secondary color— for example, red-orange and blue-violet. There are six tertiary colors, resulting in 12 colors total in the color wheel with which you may be familiar from an art class or paper scrapping.

Additionally, each color may be modified further by adding white, black, or various amounts of gray. Colors created by adding these neutral pigments are called tints, tones, and shades:

- **Tint.** Color plus white.
- **Shade.** Color plus black.
- **Tone.** Color mixed with various amounts of gray.

Once you understand color model basics, you can use color harmonies to create schemes in your layouts. Color harmonies are groups of related or complementary colors that will work together to create a pleasing arrangement. Some common color harmonies, as shown in Figure 3.13, are:

- **Monochromatic.** Shades, tints, and tones of a single color.
- **Complementary.** Color used with the color directly opposite it on the color wheel. The complement of red on a traditional color wheel is green.
- **Analogous.** Color used with the two tertiary colors adjacent to it on a color wheel. Red-orange, red, and red-yellow (or their tones, tints, and shades) would be an example of an analogous scheme.
- **Triadic.** Three colors that are equidistant from each other on the color wheel. Blue-green, yellow-orange, and red-purple are triadic colors—any tone, tint, or shade of these colors may be used to create the scheme.

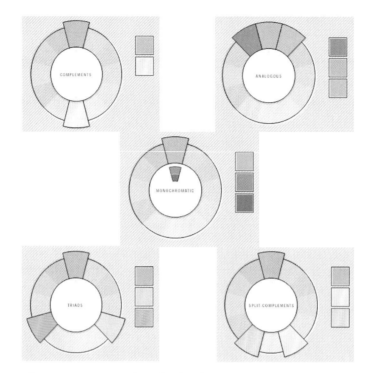

Figure 3.13 Examples of color harmonies.

◼ **Split-Complementary.** A color and the analogous colors to the right and left of that color's complement on the color wheel. Red, blue-green, and yellow-green are a split-complementary scheme.

However, computer monitors use a different color model, one based on emitted light rather than reflected light. In this model, the primary colors are red, green, and blue. This creates a bit of a dilemma if you're already familiar with the color model and wheel used by paper scrapbookers to create color schemes—you can still use the same concepts for various color harmonies, but you'll work with a RGB model instead of a RYB one.

So, what's a digital scrapper to do, if selecting co-coordinated color schemes using a computer isn't as easy as with paper and pigments? You can use a separate application to help you find good color schemes. Color Schemer Online (www.colorschemer.com/online.html) is a free Web service that will give you co-coordinating colors in either RGB or a *hexadecimal code* (or HEX, the color code you need when working with Web page colors). The tutorial at www.colorschemer.com/tutorial2.html shows you how to use this type of color layout to create traditional schemes.

The same site offers Color Schemer Studio, which adds color wheel functionality and helps you pick several design schemes (see Figure 3.14). There's a free 15-day trial of

Color Schemer Studio on the resource CD for this book. This is an excellent utility application for digital scrapbookers. It allows you to create harmonious color schemes (see Figure 3.15), save favorite color swatches, analyze how color schemes will look as

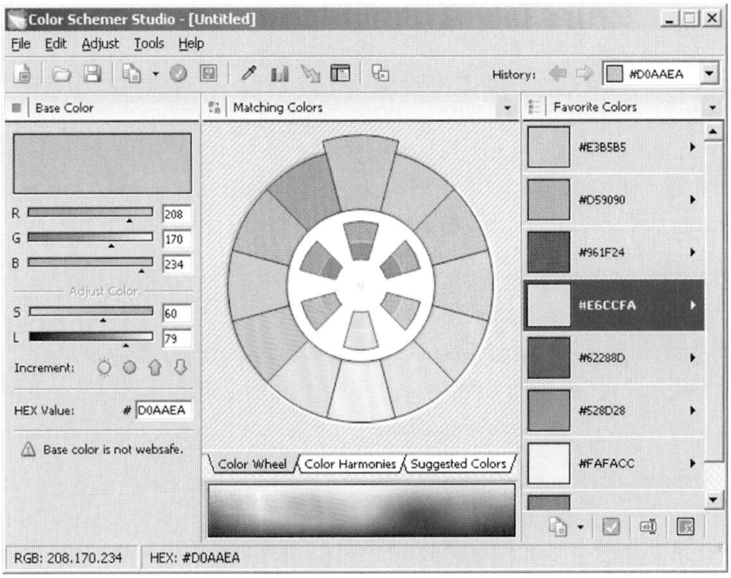

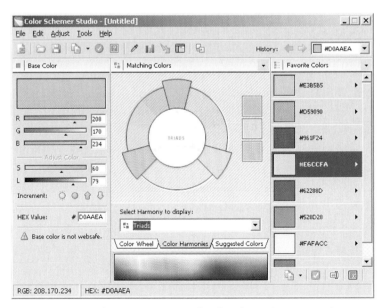

Figure 3.14 Color Wheel panel in Color Schemer Studio 1.1.

Figure 3.15 Color Harmonies tab of Color Schemer Studio 1.1.

background and text colors, and use a Suggested Colors tab to show how various color schemes will look as part of a Web page (which also works beautifully to suggest how those same colors will work in a digital layout). A triadic color scheme based on the violet base color in the left pane is shown in Figure 3.14. In the right pane, you can see a list of favorite colors created from various color harmonies and that violet color.

Once you've selected the colors you want to include in your layout, you can find their RGB or HEX color values in the Favorite Colors pane or in the bottom status bar (for the base color only). You'll need those numbers when you choose the colors in the paint program you'll use to create your layout. Color Schemer Studio can also export the Favorite Colors as well as Color Wheel, Color Mixer, and Color History colors to an Adobe Photoshop color palette, an HTML color table file, or a CSS style sheet file.

You can use a software utility to create harmonious color schemes, trust your own eyes, or use other methods. Paper scrapbookers often use ordinary paint chips, available at most hardware and paint supply stores, to reference when creating pleasing color arrangements. Digital scrappers can use these paint chips as well—just scan one in and save the image, and use it as a mini-palette of color when choosing image colors.

Color schemes can be seen all around you—in fabrics and everyday objects around the home, in nature (for who's a better colorist, the computer or Mother Nature herself?), and in the photos you use. Try to choose a color scheme that will complement the photos and not compete with them.

Creating the Basic Layout

Once you choose your color scheme, start adding it to the layout. This can be accomplished using many tools, but first you'll need to assign Background and Foreground colors.

As already noted, the concept of Background and Foreground colors is an arbitrary one (see Figure 3.16). It's just a means to have two colors readily available for use with tools such as paint brushes and flood fill tools. In Photoshop Elements 2.0, the Background and Foreground color swatches are located at the bottom of the toolbox. In Paint Shop Pro 8.1, they are located near the Color Picker in the Materials palette. PhotoPlus 9 houses the swatches on the Color tab, a floating palette which also has paint brush tips and instant effects. PhotoImpact XL adds the Background and Foreground color swatches to the toolbar.

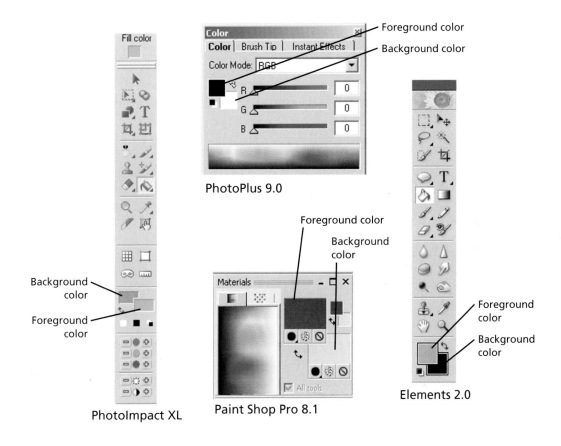

Figure 3.16 Examples of Foreground and Background Color Swatches.

In most cases, an image application can use a Flood Fill tool (usually indicated by a "paint bucket" icon) to fill an entire image or selected areas within an image. This is a quick way to fill large areas with color and to change the layout "paper" if the paint application you are using doesn't allow you to set up the layout with exactly the color background you'd like. Most applications use the current Background Color that is set to fill the image or selection. Paint Shop Pro 8.1 allows you to use either Background or Foreground colors, depending on whether you right- or left-click with the mouse when the Flood Fill tool is active. In most other applications, you can quickly switch to the Foreground color choice by clicking a button that switches the two color swatches. PhotoImpact also features a separate Fill command in the Edit menu, which will fill a background or selected area with the color, gradient, texture, or image of choice.

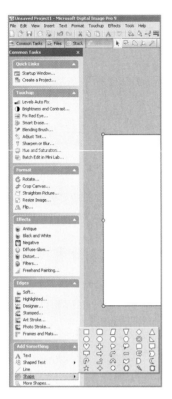

Digital Image Pro 9 does not have Background and Foreground color swatches in the traditional sense, or a traditional Flood Fill tool. However, you can create a new background color by first choosing a rectangle shape from the Add Something palette > Shape (see Figure 3.17). Drag out this rectangle by pulling at its sides, until it completely covers the image.

Click Edit > Fill with Texture or Color (see Figure 3.18). Choose the color, gradient, or image with which you'd like to fill the background.

Now you've created a layout image in the size and image resolution you want, with a colored background of your choice. Let's add some interest to that background paper now.

Figure 3.17 Digital Image Pro 9 Add a Shape.

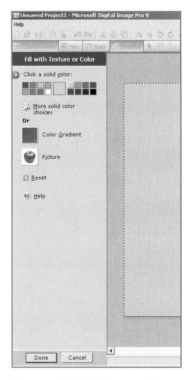

Figure 3.18 Filling an object with color in Digital Image Pro 9.

Adding Texture

All of the applications in this book have an option for adding texture to a color fill. Texture can add realism to a faux-paper layout, and creates unlimited options for presenting unique layout designs. In the layout shown in Figure 3.19, Jeri Ingalls used a sand texture fill behind the photos to simulate a beach.

Figure 3.19 "Dad at Iredale" layout by Jeri Ingalls.

Most of the applications have several tools to add many texture types, some of which can be added as part of creating the original background color. Paint Shop Pro 8.1 has a Pattern option on its Materials Editor, which is accessed by clicking any color swatch in the program, including Foreground and Background Colors. The Pattern option allows you to fill the image with colored patterns, choosing from many built-in patterns or even your own custom pattern (see Figure 3.20).

You can also add texture without additional color to an existing color fill. Check the Texture check box and access dozens of grayscale texture examples in the drop-down dialog (see Figure 3.21). This modified texture fill can be used in either the Background or Foreground color swatches, for use with the Flood Fill tool, and other tools throughout the application.

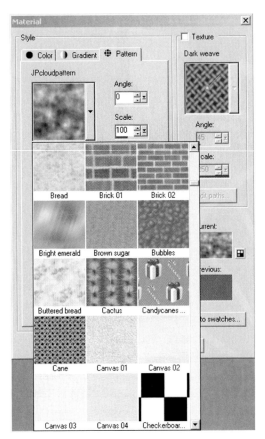

Figure 3.20 Paint Shop Pro 8.1 Materials Editor, Pattern tab.

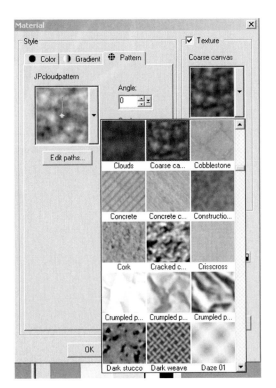

Figure 3.21 Paint Shop Pro 8.1, Texture dialog.

Paint Shop Pro 8.1 also has many texture creation effects in the Effects menu. You can choose from Stone, Leather, Mosaic, Weave, and many other effects. PhotoImpact XL has a large Natural Texture gallery in the Edit > Fill feature (see Figure 3.22).

Serif's PhotoPlus 9 also allows you to edit the fill color by adding texture. Go to Edit > Fill, change the Type to Pattern, and click the Pattern swatch to choose from a number of natural textures that can modify the fill color (see Figure 3.23).

NOTE

In many applications, it's necessary to look for a "Tolerance" setting on the Flood Fill tool. This controls how sensitive the tool is to filling areas within the image. If you are using a tool and aren't seeing any action, try setting the Tolerance setting for that tool a bit higher.

You've got the basics of your layout background. Now for the most important part— the photos! You've already prepared the photos in Chapter 2, "Digital Photo Fundamentals," so let's get them into the layout now.

In every application, the means to get these photos into the layout image involves a Copy/Paste operation. Some applications make this action very flexible by using a Layers model.

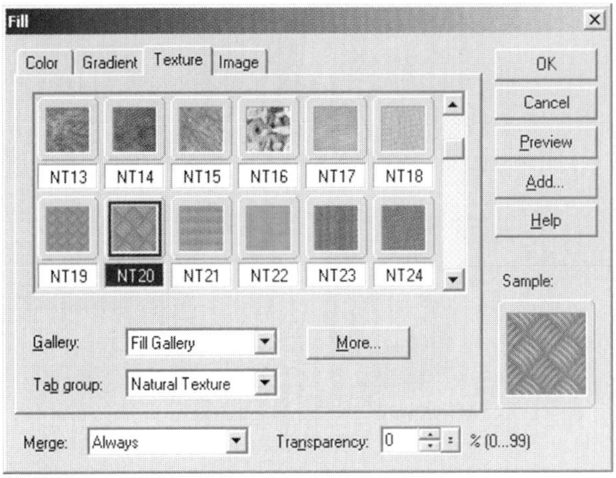

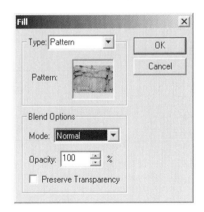

Figure 3.22 PhotoImpact XL Natural Texture gallery.

Figure 3.23 PhotoPlus 9's Pattern Fill dialog box.

NOTE

Think of Layers as layers of paper on a paper scrapbook layout, and the photos and embellishments. In a paper layout, you can move these objects around the background paper until you are satisfied. If a piece of paper rests on top of a photo, the photo is covered and can't be seen. The concept is the same with Image layers. Anything in a layer that is not transparent may cover another object below it, rendering it invisible unless the object is moved, or another action causes it to be visible. Applications that use a Layers model are flexible for the digital scrapbooker. Please refer to the Help files of your image editor for more information on Image layers.

In all the applications, you begin by opening all the photos you want to include in the layout as well as the layout image on the application workspace (see Figure 3.24). Resize the photos as needed—it's best to do this *before* you paste them into the layout, so that the application is working on a smaller image. Always work on the smallest images first, and then paste them into the layout, especially if it's a layout that uses a Layers model. Lots of layers plus high resolution equals hardworking computers!

Figure 3.24 PhotoPlus 9 workspace with layout and photos open.

NOTE

A word about Zoom view in your image editor—this allows you to reduce or enlarge the view of the image (not the image itself, an important distinction) while working on the image. You'll notice in Figure 3.24, the Zoom factor on all the images is 33%—meaning it's shown onscreen at one-third its actual size. This is helpful so that you can see the entire image. It's also helpful in determining sizes of photos and elements in relation to the layout itself and each other. Each photo is zoomed out to 33% in the workspace, as is the layout, so this gives a good hint as to the look when pasted into the layout.

Copy a photo by clicking its title bar to make it the "active" image, and use Edit > Copy to copy it to the Windows Clipboard. Return to the layout image and click the layout image's title bar to activate it. Go to Edit > Paste to paste the copied photo into the layout.

In Digital Image Pro 9, you can drag and drop an open photo image from the File Stack on the right side of the workspace (see Figure 3.25). Open the photos, create the layout, and drag the photos to the layout from the stack area. You can instantly resize the

Figure 3.25 Digital Image Pro 9 layout image with photos, File Stack area.

photos by dragging on the resize handles on the corners and sides of the photos or other objects that have been dragged or pasted into the layout.

All the applications have some sort of Mover tool. This is either a standard arrow icon or a four-headed arrow, which is used to move objects around the layout (see Figure 3.26). This can be used to move an object that's on its own layer or selections that are pasted into the layout.

Mover tool cursor

Figure 3.26 Mover tool in PhotoImpact XL.

Using Templates or Sketches

Often we have photos with which to work and no ideas. We may need a little help creating an effective layout that positions the photos in a pleasing manner or the design concept. Digital scrapbookers make good use of templates, premade layouts just waiting for you to drop your photos in, and sketches, which are design notes to help you create well-balanced layouts.

TIP

The concept of "sketches" comes from renowned scrapbook designer Becky Higgins, who creates sketches for *Creating Keepsakes* magazine as well as in her own books. *Simple Scrapbooks* magazine has its own version of "sketches" now, called "Simple Schemes."

You'll find templates from Maya and Kim Liddiard on the resource CD accompanying this book. Just open the template in your image editor, open and resize the photos you want to use, and copy/paste them into the template. Templates can be used quickly to achieve great results, and are available for free at many digital scrapbook Web sites. There are countless more templates for purchase, on CD, or by electronic download for a reasonable cost as well.

4

Adding Graphic Elements

You've prepared photos for inclusion in layouts and basic layouts for print, but now it's time for the fun stuff—adding the elements that really make scrapbooking a personal and creative endeavor. In this chapter, you'll learn how to make use of premade digital elements as well as the native tools of each application to create interesting effects. In Chapter 9, "Creating Your Own Elements," we'll show you how to create some of your own elements.

Premade digital elements can be obtained in a variety of ways. Most of the applications used in this book include at least a few tools that can quickly create photo borders and mats. Many dedicated scrapbook applications, such as Hewlett Packard's Scrapbook Assistant, Scrapbook Factory Deluxe, and Hallmark Scrapbook Studio, come with an assortment of templates, background patterns, photo mats, tags, and other decorative elements. Applications such as Paint Shop Pro and Photoshop Elements have additional program resources that make great scrapbook elements.

The most interesting elements are made by independent digital designers, and many have provided page kits and other scrapbook resources for this book. These designers specialize in creating versatile and attractive elements and page layout kits for every occasion, ready to use as is or modified to meet your own needs. There are many types of premade elements available, including full-page templates, which are usually complete layouts with elements already in position, needing only photos to be added. Many designers offer complete sets of individual elements, some with full-sized page backgrounds as well as patterns for you to create your own background papers. You'll also find decorative alphabets so you can create custom titles (see Figure 4.1).

Figure 4.1 Page layouts by Lauren Bavin and Sally Beacham.
Layout kits by Lauren Bavin and Tracy Pori.

Some designers offer free elements and whole page kits at Web sites, such as www.digitalscrapbookplace.com, and through e-mail lists and newsgroups. It's possible to create an entire collection of digital scrapbook resources for nothing but the time and expense of downloading them to your computer. In addition, many designers offer page layout kits for download at a reasonable cost or individual elements that can be purchased individually and reused again and again. You'll find a list of Web sites that offer both free and retail digital scrapbook designs in this book's Appendix A section.

The resource CD for this book contains page layout kits from Lauren Bavin, Angela Cable, Janice "Maya" Dye-Szucs, Kim Liddiard, Margie Lundy, Tracy Pori, and Jenna Robertson. You'll notice completed layouts by some of those designers sprinkled throughout the book. Feel free to use those illustrations as inspiration to create your own masterpiece. You can also combine elements from one kit with another, and then colorize or resize as needed.

If you're undecided as to which image-editing software application might be best for you, this chapter (along with Chapters 2 and 7, the photo-editing chapters) may help you decide, based on the features offered. After all, you'll create the best digital layouts with great layouts that enhance your photos and present your own unique perspective. Happy hunting!

The Photographs

In Chapter 2, "Digital Photo Fundamentals," you learned how to edit and enhance photos, and Chapter 3, "Basic Layout Guidelines," included basic information about pasting those photos into your layout image. Now you'll add some interest to your photos by adding mats, frames, and edge effects. In Chapter 7, "Advanced Photo Techniques," you'll learn how to create artistic enhancements to the photos themselves, but for now you'll add border and edge effects. You'll use some of the native application tools as well as premade elements from several of the most creative digital scrapbook designers.

Photo Mats and Borders

First, add one of the most basic effects—a photo border. Older film snapshots, as well as Polaroids, often have a white border when printed and most digital images lack that, so you may wish to add one, for realism's sake. Most of the applications have a tool or feature to create a border quickly, or at least fairly easily, and some make creating special frame effects a breeze.

In Paint Shop Pro 8.1, go to Image > Add Borders (see Figure 4.2). You can choose to add symmetric borders on every side, as well as color and width. Border widths can be set in inches, centimeters, or pixels.

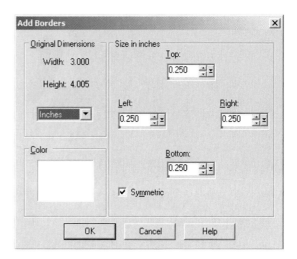

Figure 4.2 Add Borders dialog box in Paint Shop Pro 8.1.

Photoshop Elements 2.0 can add a border in a couple ways, although not directly with a border creation tool. Let's start by setting the Foreground color in the color picker to the desired border color. Go to Image > Resize > Canvas Size (see Figure 4.3). You can choose from an impressive number of measurement units, including percent, pixels, inches, and centimeters.

You'll have to do a little math here—if you want a quarter-inch border on every side, add a half-inch to the height and width of the current image to gain the new image dimensions. Center the image by depressing the button in the middle of the positioning panel (see Figure 4.4).

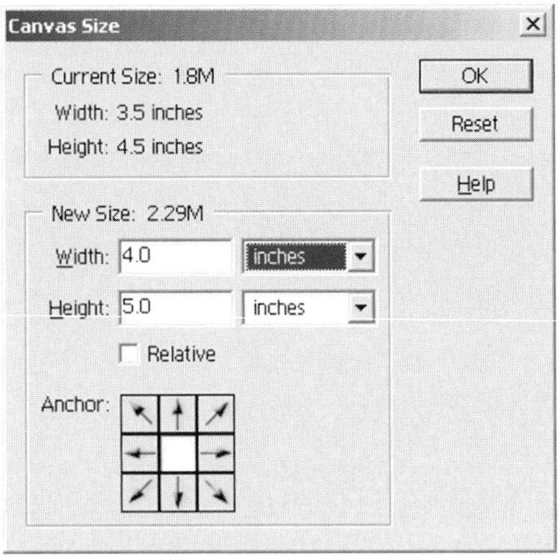

Figure 4.3 Canvas Size dialog box in Photoshop Elements 2.0.

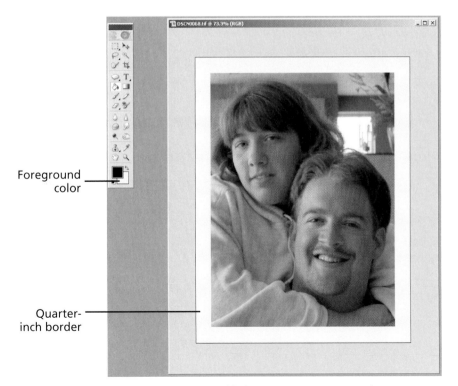

Foreground color

Quarter-inch border

Figure 4.4 Border added using Canvas Resize feature.

You can also add an additional border effect by using the Edit > Stroke command. First, you have to select the entire image, so go to Select > Select All. This will place a blinking "marquee" around the image perimeter, indicating that everything in the image is selected so that any effect or tool applies to the entire image. Now go to Edit > Stroke. Here you can define a *stroke*, a path around the outside of an object, to apply on the outside, center, or inside of a selection. You can't apply it to the outside of this selection because that will place it outside the image boundaries and thus be invisible. You can set the width in pixels, as shown in Figure 4.5, or in inches by entering a value such as ".25 in," which results in a stroke width of a quarter-inch on all four sides.

Serif's PhotoPlus 9 uses a similar convention as Elements to add a plain border, although you'll need to increase the canvas size. Go to Image > Canvas Size and set the new image dimensions to include the border, and click the position button to center the image (see Figure 4.6). The foreground color in the color palette will be used as the new canvas border.

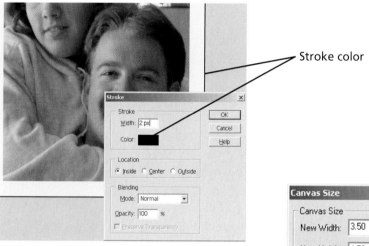

Figure 4.5 Border added using Edit > Stroke command.

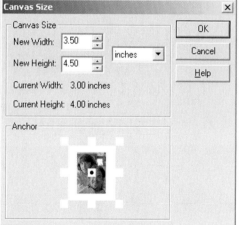

Figure 4.6 Increasing canvas size in PhotoPlus 9.

PhotoImpact XL does include a border command, but it won't add a border *outside* a photo's existing edges without a little work. This means, once again, you'll have to increase the canvas size. Go to Format > Expand Canvas (see Figure 4.7). You can set the new canvas color, but you'll have to choose the border width in pixel dimensions. If you're working at an image of 200 pixels per inch, a quarter-inch border on one side would equate to 50 pixels. Check the Expand sides equally check box to create symmetric borders by entering one border's value only.

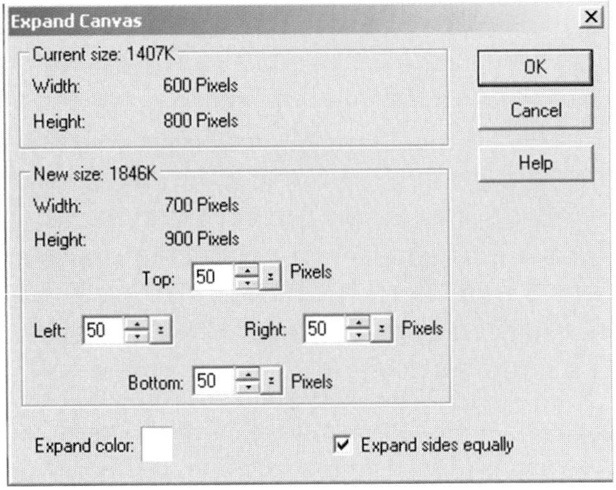

Figure 4.7 Expanding canvas size in PhotoImpact XL.

If you'd like to add a border that covers some of the existing photo edge, you can use PhotoImpact XL's Border command (see Figure 4.8). Begin by selecting the entire image, and then go to Selection > All. You'll see a selection marquee around the entire photo. Right-click the image itself, and choose Border from the menu. Again, set the dimensions in pixels, and choose the Inward option. Fill the newly created border with the color of your choice. The only advantage to using this tool over the Expand Canvas Size method is the ability to add rounded corners to the border and a soft edge.

Figure 4.8 Border command in PhotoImpact XL.

Creating Edge Effects

Digital Image Pro 9 offers an impressive number of edge, frame, border, and mat options, but to add a simple white border, you'll have to go to Format > Resize Canvas (see Figure 4.9). Select the new canvas size to include the border width you'd like, and position the photo in the center of it using the pushpin icon. Click Done when you're satisfied with the border.

Let's talk about some of those built-in frame and mat effects now. Digital Image Pro 9 has an extensive array of options—many of them contained in the Edges palette on the left side of the workspace (see Figure 4.10).

You can choose from Soft, Highlighted, Designer, and Frames and Mat edges as well as Stamped, Photo Stroke, and Art Stroke edges—specialized tools to create fun or unique effects. Figure 4.11 shows the example photo with a realistic rope border effect added.

Figure 4.9 Border added using Resize Canvas command.

Figure 4.10 Edges palette in Digital Image Pro 9.

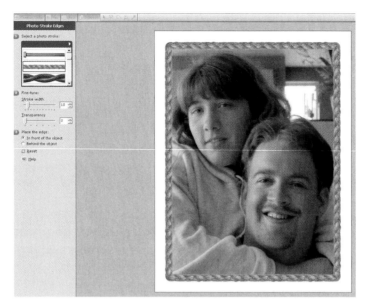

Figure 4.11 Photo Stroke Edges in Digital Image Pro 9.

Paint Shop Pro 8.1 has a number of similar features to add fancy edges and frames. Go to Image > Picture Frame to find a slew of built-in frames and mats (see Figure 4.12). There are a number of options in this dialog box to allow you to customize frames to work with your particular photo.

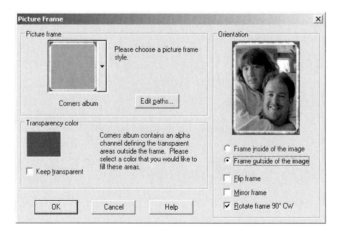

Figure 4.12 Paint Shop Pro's Picture Frame tool.

PhotoImpact XL includes a Stamp tool that can be used to create interesting frame effects (see Figure 4.13). Activate the Stamp tool and you can set the brush size, various options for placing the objects in the Stamp file, as well as the type of path to which those objects are applied.

PhotoImpact XL also has a Frame option at Format > Frame and Shadow. Click the Frame tab and you'll see a terrific number of styles, with many options to modify size, color, texture, and shape.

Another common edge style that's useful is the vignette—this is a soft, feathered edge that blends into another background, either solid or patterned. This effect is also useful in creating photo montages.

A feathered edge is usually produced as part of applying a selection shape to an image. Higher feather settings produce softer edges and wider transition areas between a photo and background. Some applications allow you to modify the feather setting after you apply it, but most require you to set the feather setting before you define the selection.

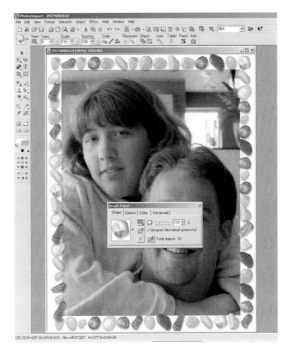

Figure 4.13 Photo frame effect created with PhotoImpact XL's Stamp tool.

Open a photo in PhotoPlus 9. Activate the Shape Selection tool, set it to the Ellipse, and set the Feather amount in the Tool Options palette to a pixel amount. I used 25 pixels in Figure 4.14 as a good amount to feather, on an image that is about 800×950 pixels. Drag out the selection on the photo and position it where you like.

Once the selection is properly positioned, invert it! Inverting (reversing) a selection is just as useful as creating one in the first place—what was previously *not* selected becomes selected. To invert a selection in PhotoPlus 9, go to Select > Invert. You'll see the marquee now includes the outside border as well as an ellipse (see Figure 4.15). Don't be confused, the actual ellipse is not selected, it becomes a "hole" in the actual selection. Now you can delete the contents of this selection (press the Delete key, or go to Edit > Clear, which will replace the photo bits with the current background color set in PhotoPlus's Color Picker).

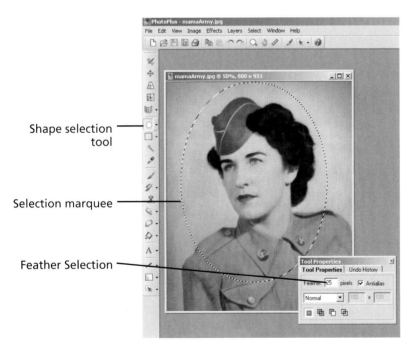

Shape selection tool

Selection marquee

Feather Selection

Figure 4.14 Feathered selection in PhotoPlus 9.

Figure 4.15 Vignette effect in PhotoPlus 9.

The technique works exactly the same way in Photoshop Elements 2.0. Choose the Ellipse Selection Marquee, set the feather in the tool options, drag out the selection and position it, invert the selection (go to Select > Inverse), and delete the selection contents. The current background color is used to fill the selection.

The action may look a little different in Digital Image Pro 9, but the concept remains the same. Open an image. Click the Marquee tool in the toolbar (see Figure 4.16). If you cannot see the Marquee Tool options palette, go to View > Selection Options and toggle it on by clicking that menu entry. Click the Shape options in the palette—you have more than 50 shape selection options from which to choose. It's possible to adjust the shape, set the feather, and invert the selection directly from the palette.

All the applications covered in this book allow you to create your own edge effects—some more easily than others. They also allow you to create a transparent background, so that you can layer that image over another background or image with no edges showing. In most applications, if you have the option to create the image on a transparent background, you can copy the selected vignette out of the image and paste it into a layout or new image.

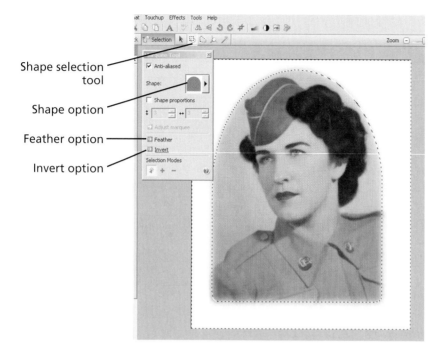

Shape selection tool

Shape option

Feather option

Invert option

Figure 4.16 Digital Image Pro 9's Selection tools.

Color My World

For any digital scrapbooker, a technique to learn well is how to recolor a digital element. One of the basic advantages of digital scrapbooking is that you'll *always* have paper and embellishments to match any photo or existing layout. A gold eyelet doesn't have to be gold for long!

To demonstrate how easy this can be, open an image from the CD collection of goodies. You can choose any element you want from the various kits on the CD, but the gray glass bead image from Tracy Pori's Licorice kit is used here. This bead is a medium-gray, which makes it a good candidate to colorize. Many of the applications have specialized tools for correcting color, but we'll go the simple route.

All of the applications have a means to change color, or colorize, by modifying an existing color's hue, saturation, or lightness values:

■ **PhotoImpact XL.** Go to Format > Hue and Saturation. Click the button marked Colorize, and then adjust the sliders to change the color of the image. Check the Preview box to see the color change updated on the image in real time as well as in the Preview pane on the right side.

- **Paint Shop Pro 8.1.** Go to Adjust > Hue and Saturation > Colorize. Move the sliders to adjust the hue and saturation values. Click the Auto Proof icon to see the change updated on the image as well as in the Preview pane on the right side.
- **Digital Image Pro 9.** Go to Touchup > Adjust Tint. Move the Color and Amount sliders to colorize.
- **Photoshop Elements 2.0.** Go to Enhance > Adjust Color > Hue and Saturation. Check the Colorize and Preview boxes. Move the Hue, Saturation, and Lightness sliders to change the color of the image.
- **PhotoPlus 9.** Identical to Photoshop Elements 2.0. Go to Image > Adjust > Hue/Saturation/Lightness. Check the Colorize and Preview boxes and move the sliders to colorize the image.

The colored beads in Figure 4.17 are all created from that single gray glass bead, in each of the applications.

There are other tools to selectively recolor elements. In each application, look for features or tools that modify hue, saturation, lightness, tint, color balance, color cast, or features that remove or replace colors. Paint Shop Pro 8.1 has a special Manual Color Correction tool that can modify an image's color with an entire catalog of built-in colors, or by manually selecting a new color and shifting the rest of the colors in the image in the same way (see Figure 4.18).

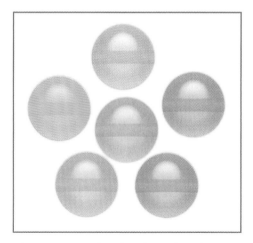

Figure 4.17 Glass bead recolored in various applications.

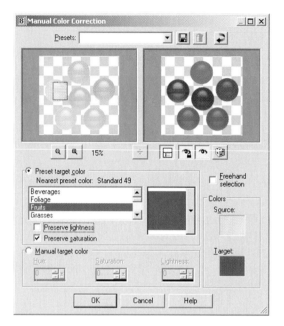

Figure 4.18 Manual Color Correction tool in Paint Shop Pro 8.1.

You can recolor portions of elements by selecting the area you want colored. We've used shape selection tools in each application so far, but there are often other types of selection tools, including freehand *lasso* and *Magic Wand* tools. Freehand tools usually allow you to draw custom selections around an object. Magic Wand selection tools usually select areas of the image by color, or some facet of color such as RGB value, hue, brightness, or opacity.

Photo Frames

Next, you'll create some framed and matted photos for use in your layouts. On the resource CD, open the layout kit from Lauren Bavin titled "Album" kit. You'll find wooden backgrounds for 12 × 12 inch and 8 × 10 inch layouts, a manila folder, photo album, paper clips, buttons, rivets, thumbtacks, torn paper, photo corners, a book plate, and tools. In short, images of common items people use to create a scrapbook (see Figure 4.19).

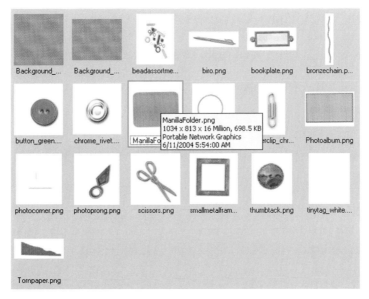

Figure 4.19 Lauren Bavin's "Album" kit images.

First, build the smaller elements of the final layout. It may help to sketch out the way you want the layout to look ahead of time—what large elements and photos should be placed where on the finished size layout. Not to worry, everything is infinitely movable in a digital layout. There's no glue to dry!

Open the photos you'd like to use, and prepare them for the layout, sizing them to the scale you want to use. Now choose a mat for these photos. From the "Album" kit files, choose the ManilaFolder.png file and open it in the image editor you're using.

This image is actually a large photo mat, for positioning a photo or two on top before placement in the full-size layout. Copy the photos you'd like to "lay" on top of the mat into that image:

- **PhotoImpact XL.** With the photo image active, go to Edit > Copy. Make the mat image active, and go to Edit > Paste > Paste under Pointer. This will activate the Pick tool temporarily, so you can position the photo where you would like it on the mat. Use the Transform tool to resize, reshape, and rotate as needed. There are many rotation and transformation methods on the Tool Options palette.

- **Paint Shop Pro 8.1.** With the photo image active, go to Edit > Copy. Make the mat image active, and go to Edit > Paste > Paste as New Layer. Use the Mover tool (the four-headed arrow) to move the photo into the proper position on the mat. Use the Deform tool to resize, reshape, and rotate as needed.

- **Digital Image Pro 9.** With the photo image as the active image in the Files panel, click the Object Selection tool (the arrow) in the Selections toolbar. Click the photo image to select it. Go to Edit > Copy. Click the mat image in the Files panel. Go to Edit > Paste. Position, scale, and rotate as needed.

- **Photoshop Elements 2.0.** With the photo image active, go Select > Select All, and then to Edit > Copy. Make the mat image active, and go to Edit > Paste. Use the Move tool (the arrow) to move the photo into the proper position on the mat. Go to Image > Transform > Free Transform to resize, reshape, and rotate as needed.

- **PhotoPlus 9.** With the photo image active, go to Edit > Copy. Make the mat image active, and go to Edit > Paste > As New Layer. Use the Mover tool (the four-headed arrow) to move the photo into the proper position on the mat. Use the Deform tool to resize, reshape, and rotate as needed.

Once you have the photos positioned, the mat is almost complete (see Figure 4.20).

Figure 4.20 Photos positioned on "Manila Folder" mat.

Creating Depth and Realism

It's important for faux paper-style scrapbooking to create an illusion of realism—elements should look as "real" as possible. Adding shadows to create depth will help create this aura of realism (see Figure 4.21). You'll add some shadows around your photos to lift them off the manila folder:

- **PhotoImpact XL.** Click one of the photos to select it in the mat image. Go to Format > Frame & Shadow, click the Shadow Tab, and check the Shadow check box to add a shadow to the frame. Adjust the available options for size, transparency, softness, and color. Click OK to apply the shadow. Repeat for any other photos.

- **Paint Shop Pro 8.1.** Click one of the photos with the Mover tool. The photo will be the active layer in Paint Shop Pro's Layers palette. Go to Effects > 3D Effects > Drop Shadow. Adjust the available options for opacity, blur, and color as well as the offsets for size and positioning. You can choose to apply the shadow on its own layer, which will also be linked to the object's layer. Click OK to apply the shadow. Repeat for any other photos.

- **Digital Image Pro 9.** Click one of the photos. Go to Effects > Shadow. From the dialog box, select one of the preset shadow options, and then click Customize if the shadow isn't exactly what you want. In the Shadow dialog box, you can set the color, transparency, and softness options. Click and drag the bounding box around the photo to modify the shadow size and height. Click Done to apply.

- **Photoshop Elements 2.0.** Click one of the photos. Open the Layer Styles palette, and choose the Shadows category. Select a layer style and drag it over to the image. Drop it on top of the photo you wish to shadow. To customize it, go to Layer > Layer Style > Style Settings. In the dialog box, you'll find options to set the Lighting Angle and the Shadow Distance. Click OK to apply.

- **PhotoPlus 9.** Click one of the photos with the Mover tool. Go to Layers > Effects. The Layer Effects dialog box opens. Check the Drop Shadow check box, and then set the light angle, color, opacity, blur, distance, and intensity of the shadow. Click OK to apply.

Figure 4.21 Drop Shadows applied to photos on mat.

TIP

Drop and perspective shadows consist of direction, color, transparency, size or width, and blur or softness. The direction of the shadow should be determined by the placement of a theoretical light source shining on the object. For example, if the sun is shining on an object from the upper-right corner of an image, the shadow on the object should primarily show in the bottom-left quadrant of the image, away from the light source. Light directly in front of an image would throw a cast shadow, behind the image. It's important to keep the shadow direction consistent in the whole layout, so keep this in mind if you are creating elements outside the layout to be pasted in later. You don't want the shadow in one direction on one element, and an opposing direction on another!

The size of the shadow indicates how far an object is away from another object behind it, and the blur or softness indicates how far the object is away from the light source itself. An object directly in front of a bright light source would have a hard-edged shadow. An object with a wider or larger size shadow setting would appear to be higher off the background than a smaller size shadow setting.

Tags and Banners

Once you've got photos prepared for your layout, you can choose additional design elements. Tags and banners are important elements of scrapbook design because they hold much of the text and journaling. Text is covered in Chapter 5, "Text Techniques," but we'll examine tags now.

NOTE

> You have the start of an extensive collection of elements on this book's CD, but you'll likely collect and create many more. You'll probably find it convenient to browse the image files using an image browser in the image editor you're using. Most of the applications in this book have integrated image browsers, often accessed through the program's File menu. Digital Image Pro 9 doesn't have an integrated browser, but it can be purchased in a suite with Digital Image Library, which can be used to archive and manage your images.

The Eraser brush is the one tool most useful for modifying premade tags and assembling more complex images. With it, you can erase bits of objects that are layered over other objects, revealing the area beneath and creating a 3D illusion. In Figure 4.22, the area of the paperclip that lays over the chain link is erased, making it appear that the clip is looped through the link. To do this yourself, open bronzechain.png, paperclip_chrome.png, and tinytag_white.png from Lauren's "Album" kit on the CD:

1. Create a new image, 6 × 3 inches, 200 pixels per inch resolution, with a transparent background. Make the bronzechain.png image active and copy it (Edit > Copy, in most cases). Return to the new image and paste the chain image into it, as a new layer or object.

2. Rotate the chain 90°, so that it's horizontal in the new image.

3. Copy and paste the paperclip image into the new image, as a new layer or object. Align the paperclip over the chain, as if the clip is dangling from the chain.

4. Use the Eraser tool to erase the bit of the clip that overlays one section of the chain link, as shown in Figure 4.22.

5. Continue pasting paperclips into the new image. Use the Deform or Transform tools to vary the angle of the paperclips that dangle from the chain. Use the Eraser brush to erase just enough of the paperclip to simulate its attachment to the chain.

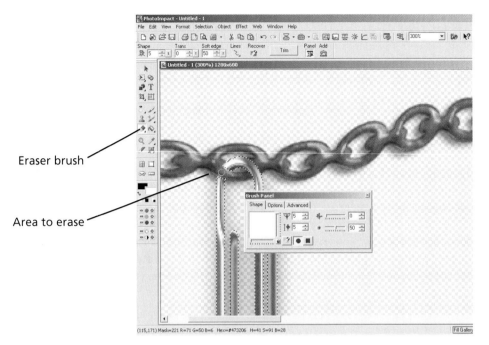

Eraser brush

Area to erase

Figure 4.22 Paperclip image attached to bronze chain with Eraser tool in PhotoImpact XL.

You can build complex tag elements from simple elements. In Figure 4.23, tiny white tags are added to the chain/paperclip element, in the same fashion as the paperclips. Drop shadows were added to all the tags as well after they were positioned on the paperclips.

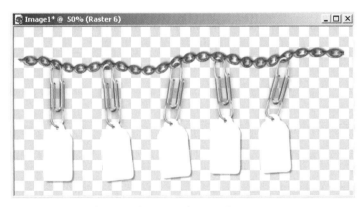

Figure 4.23 Chain with paperclips and paper tags in Paint Shop Pro 8.1.

Once you've completed a complex element, save it for later use, and then merge the layers, if possible. (It's always good to have a backup copy.) This will reduce file size and destress your computer resources when you paste the whole element into the final layout image. However, once you've merged the layers, you won't be able to make any changes in position of the elements because the entire image will become "fixed":

- **PhotoImpact XL.** Object > Merge All.
- **Paint Shop Pro 8.1.** Layers > Merge > Merge Visible.
- **Digital Image Pro 9.** Edit > Flatten > Flatten All Objects.
- **Photoshop Elements 2.0.** Layer > Merge > Merge Visible.
- **PhotoPlus 9.** Layers > Merge Visible.

In the "Album" kit used in this chapter, you'll find a bookplate, a plain white tag, and various bits and baubles. Also on the CD, Tracy Pori's "Licorice" layout kit has several plain and metal-rimmed tags, some of them with transparent vellum centers. You'll discover lots of tags, pockets, and envelopes throughout the kit folders. Remember, you can colorize just about any element or paper to match other designs.

Ribbons, Fibers, and Bows, Oh My!

Paper scrapbookers have embraced the concept of *lumpy layouts*—this means adding dimension and texture to a layout by adding objects that "lift" off the page, such as ribbons, yarn, fabric, and other common crafter's notions. The digital scrapbooker can emulate that look, without the bulk and weight added to a paper page. (This bulk can cause storage dilemmas as well as potentially affect the archival life of any photos included in layouts with those types of decorations.)

In the CD resource files for this book, you'll find ribbons, fuzzy fibers, chains, and rickrack trims. Have fun choosing, modifying, and colorizing!

Embellishments and Elements

Adding decorative elements to your layout can result in a truly creative and unique image, and is perhaps the most exciting aspect of scrapbooking. You can choose from a variety of embellishments so that no layout looks like any other layout, even when using the same papers and mats.

Paper scrapbookers refer to the decorative elements added to their pages as *embellishments*. Digital scrapbookers refer to embellishments as *elements*. Elements can include, but aren't limited to, things like stickers; clip art; metal eyelets; brads and snaps; metal and plastic mesh; clear glass or plastic pebbles; metal, wood, or plastic frames and plaques; and slide mounts and coin holders—the list goes on and on! You can create many of these elements yourself, using several of the image editors covered in this book. Some applications even include premade resources that can be used. For example, Web graphic buttons can be modified to look like real buttons or page pebbles. Mesh patterns can be used to create metallic mesh.

Of course, you can purchase digital elements or find plenty of free ones on the Internet, but you can also create your own (see Chapter 9, "Creating Your Own Elements," for fun with that idea). You can also use your scanner to come up with unique papers and embellishments from everyday objects—scan in buttons, shells, old jewelry, macaroni shapes, and toys, you name it!

The book's CD contains eyelets of various types and finishes, buttons, beads, charms, and watch pieces. Lauren Bavin's "Time Flies" layout kit is shown in Figure 4.24. Browse through the files to find all sorts of treasures. Images from one kit can easily be modified to work with elements from another.

Open these images and copy/paste them into your layout, just as we did with the photos and tag elements earlier in the chapter. Use the Deform or Transform tool (or a feature like this) to move them into place, resizing and rotating if necessary. Remember

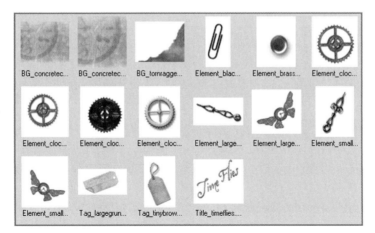

Figure 4.24 "Time Flies" layout kit images from Lauren Bavin.

to colorize if something doesn't quite match the color scheme with which you're working! Add shadows as necessary, keeping the direction of the shadows consistent for the most realistic look.

Figure 4.25 shows a completed layout, using elements from the "Album" kit. We've used the 12×12 inch wooden background paper as the layout's background image, and added the album element, the completed manila folder photo mat, the chain with paperclips and tags, as well as another photo with photo corners and some elements sprinkled around for authenticity. Some of the elements come complete with their own shadows, but additional shadows were added to each object as needed.

Figure 4.25 "Twins" layout by Sally Beacham, "Album" kit from Lauren Bavin.

Using Digital Elements on Paper Layouts

Thus far we've discussed creating totally digital pages, but you can also add a touch of digital creativity to paper scrapbook layouts. Clip art makes wonderful stickers when printed on sticker paper or clear label sheets. If printed on sticker paper, you'll want to trim closely to the printed edges. If you print on clear sticker labels (which are available in many sizes, including whole 8.5×11 inch sheets), you won't need to worry about trimming so closely, as the clear sticker material itself will be virtually invisible, especially inside a plastic layout protector in an album.

Anything that you can create for a digital layout, you can print out to add to a paper layout as well. Consider matting your photos in your image editor, and printing them out as one piece. The "lumpy bumpy" embellishments you love to see can become part of a neat, flat paper layout, if you print out digital versions and adhere them to your traditional layouts. You'll never run out of the perfect embellishment again—once you've created, purchased, or downloaded that great digital embellishment, you can use it over and over again, in a size and color perfectly suited to the layout.

5

Text Techniques

The second most important concept of scrapbooking involves words—using titles and journaling to tell the story. In some cases, finding the right words may be a difficult task, but presenting those words in myriad ways is easy, using your computer. In fact, many traditional paper scrapbookers use computer-generated text almost exclusively in their paper layouts. If you aren't fond of your own handwriting, and don't want to invest your children's inheritance in alphabet stickers and letter tiles, computer journaling makes the most sense. In Figure 5.1, computer journaling on vellum paper is used to mimic the type style in the title block, snipped from a cruise activities newsletter.

If you'd like to use computer journaling with your traditional paper layouts, you can print text on a separate piece of paper, trim it, layer it over the title area, and use adhesive or glue-dots to give it a 3D look. You can use most cardstock and other paper types, and even some handmade papers work well in inkjet printers. In addition, you can use transparent vellum, which is pretty, especially layered over a patterned paper or photo. However, it's hard to adhere vellum by itself because the adhesive often shows through. In that case, you might consider attaching your vellum paper to the paper layout using a metal eyelet or brad. Another trick for a vellum title box is to hide the area where the adhesive shows through the vellum by layering other non-transparent paper over that area. Vellum may require a little more time to dry than regular paper.

You can create your own word and photo transparencies—the kind that cost several dollars at scrapbook stores. Do this by buying inkjet transparency sheets and printing words and phrases or images using the manufacturer's suggested ink and drying time.

Figure 5.1 "Labadee" traditional paper layout by Sally Beacham.

Text is important in every layout, even those that only have a title. It's integral to a style of scrapbooking known as *Word Art* or *graphic-style*. Generally, a layout in this style has few embellishments, and isn't meant to simulate a paper scrapbook layout. This style creates a layout that resembles something you'd see in a glossy magazine advertisement. In fact, the inspiration for many graphic-style pages comes from magazines and commercials, or from paintings and other artwork. Amanda Behrmann, partner/designer at www.digitalscrapbookplace.com, used fonts to great effect in the graphic-style layout shown in Figure 5.2.

All of the applications used in this book allow the user to create text in countless ways. Some applications have more built-in features than others, but each will allow you to customize the text you want to add to your layouts.

Finding Fonts

Fonts, wonderful fonts! For every scrapbook layout, there's a font (or 100) that coordinates beautifully, matching mood and style of the design. Finding the perfect font is every bit as addictive as seeking out the elements that make your layout special.

Figure 5.2 "Hello" layout, courtesy Amanda Behrmann. Fonts used—Bookman Old Style and CK Journaling.

Freeware Fonts

It's not necessary to spend a lot of money to start a great collection of fonts. Many of the applications you already own come with a number of fonts. PhotoPlus comes with bonus fonts on a resource CD included with the program. CorelDRAW and Xara X have a number of excellent fonts on their installation CDs, so check out software that you already own. In addition, card creator and desktop publishing programs usually contain a number of fonts.

In Figure 5.3, Ron Lacey used an Esselte font called Papyrus to create this panoramic layout; this font is often included in a number of Microsoft applications. This is a perfect example of a graphic-style layout—a great photo, expressive journaling, and a bold title.

Figure 5.3 "The Land of the Sleeping Giant" panorama by Ron Lacey. Font used—Papyrus.

The Internet is a treasure chest of fonts—check out this book's Appendix A for font resources on the Web. However, be advised that not all fonts are free. Many fonts are shareware, meaning you can test drive them to see if you like them, but if you'd like to keep them, you should pay for them.

Goodies on the CD

This book's CD contains fonts from Larabie Fonts, House of Lime, and Typadelic, free for your use. Ronna Penner, font designer for Typadelic, used computer-generated fonts for the cover of this altered book journal shown in Figure 5.4, including her own Not Too Shabby font, which can be found

Figure 5.4 Altered book journal by Ronna Penner, using fonts from T-26, P22, and her own Not Too Shabby font from Typadelic.

on the resource CD. Ronna's journal is a great example of using computer-generated text in a primarily traditional paper art format.

Kim Liddiard used the Larabie font Euphorigenic as the title for this Word Art-style layout in Figure 5.5. You can find 100 Larabie fonts on the CD, in classic as well as fun and funky typeface styles. Kim's layout utilizes just a simple title, with repeated vertical text.

Searching the Web

Use just about any Internet search engine (Google, Yahoo, or Dogpile) to search for "fonts" and you'll find more links than you'll ever be able to research! Scrapbook sites have whole font sections, with some available for download and some available on CDs that can be purchased online or through a local scrapbook store. Some well-known

Figure 5.5 "Happiness" layout, courtesy Kim Liddiard. Font used—Euphorigenic from Larabie fonts.

commercial scrapbooking font sites include 2Peas in a Bucket (www.twopeasinabucket.net) and Creating Keepsakes (www.creatingkeepsakes.com). You can download fonts from many Web sites—they're often posted as compressed ZIP files, or in the case of Macintosh (Mac) fonts, as SIT files. Windows XP operating system includes a ZIP utility to extract these files. For older Windows operating systems, you'll need a compression application such as WinZip (www.winzip.com). Mac users will need a Mac application like StuffIt (www.stuffit.com). Download the font files to a folder on your computer. We'll talk about actually installing fonts a little later in the chapter.

Commercial Fonts

Font foundries offer commercial versions of their fonts, and some for reasonable prices. Why pay for a font when there are so many free fonts available? Most commercial fonts come in *families*, which include various weights and styles of the same font—bold, italic, wide, condensed, etc. They're usually developed with great care and attention paid to small details. They also often include extended character sets with extra symbols and special characters. If you have a special project such as a wedding album, you may want to invest in a special font (one that you won't see everywhere), that will add a distinctive touch to your most precious projects.

In Figure 5.6, Jeri Ingalls used Phyllis Initials from URW, a beautiful script font with fancy initials. This font is available at various font sites for about US$20.

Entire books can be devoted to the concept of font design; a brief synopsis of typefaces follows:

- **Serif-style fonts.** Have small horizontal lines on the ends of vertical letter strokes. Serif fonts aid reading legibility as the eye follows the serif from one letter to the next.

- **San-serif fonts.** Lack serifs. May not be as easy to read, but can add a lot of impact to a title or subheading.

- **Script fonts.** Can be formal or informal. Some script fonts resemble handwriting and can be appropriate for journaling.

- **Specialty fonts.** Often have small decorative characters incorporated in the font, such as flowers, snowflakes, hearts, and ladybugs.

- **Dingbat fonts.** Fonts that are actually images, not letters or numbers. Dingbats are great for creating your own clip art!

Figure 5.6 "Winter Webs" layout by Jeri Ingalls. Fonts used—Phyllis Initials from URW.

Many fonts don't come in these family variations, however, most image editors and word processing applications allow you to simulate these font style attributes with Bold, Italic, Strikethrough, and Underline options. Even if a bold version of the font already exists, such as Arial Black, applying the Bold option will make the font even bolder.

Computer Fonts with Die-Cut Alphabets

Of particular interest to scrapbookers are fonts that are similar to a popular portable die-cut system called Quickutz. This is a hand tool that uses small metal dies to punch out paper letters that are then adhered to paper layouts. If you're interested in creating digital layouts that simulate paper layouts, you might want to have a collection of fonts that match the Quickutz alphabet dies. It's also a good idea if you are a traditional paper scrapbooker—the Quickutz dies only come in a couple sizes, so you don't have much flexibility with the titles you can create with the die-cut letters. By combining the die-cut letters with computer-generated titles and journaling, you can have any size you want.

Some font styles can be printed, cut out with scissors, and added to a page. Another workaround is to print the text on clear sticker paper, and then adhere it to the layout. Of course, if you're doing a completely digital layout, you can emulate the look of the Quickutz fonts easily (and no scissors are needed at all).

Table 5.1 shows the Quickutz alphabet styles currently available, and the fonts that are equivalent to them. Some are readily available as freeware, and others are commercial fonts you'll have to pay for, but you'll be able to use them over and over again, to match or simulate your Quickutz alphabet dies!

Table 5.1 Quickutz font equivalents

Quickutz Alphabet Die Set	*True Type Font Equivalent*
Honey	Chauncy Fatty
Star	Comic Strip Poster
Marisa	Lucida Handwriting
Sonja	Rage Italic
Indigo	Ondine
Venus	Ravie
Khaki	Benderville
Zelda	Jokerman
Roxy	Showcard Moderne
Paige	Garamouche
Sophie	Chocolate Mint Surprise
Gidget	Pen Tip DT Bold
Eliza	P22 Victorian Swash
Empire	Rusticana
Phoebe	Limehouse Script
Frankie	Snoopy Snails NF

Installing and Using Fonts

Some folks collect fonts like others collect shoes, or clip art. Windows XP can handle hundreds of installed fonts, but older operating systems sometimes balk if you have more than 200 or so installed fonts. However, it's not necessary to actually install a font to use it in many applications. You can download and unzip a font to a folder, click the font file to open it (see Figure 5.7), and minimize it to your taskbar.

Go to your image application and look in your font drop-down dialog box—the font will appear in the list as long as you have it open on your computer, and will be available for use. Once you close it, the font will disappear from the application's drop-down font list. This little trick works in all the image editors covered in this book, except for Digital Image Pro 9.

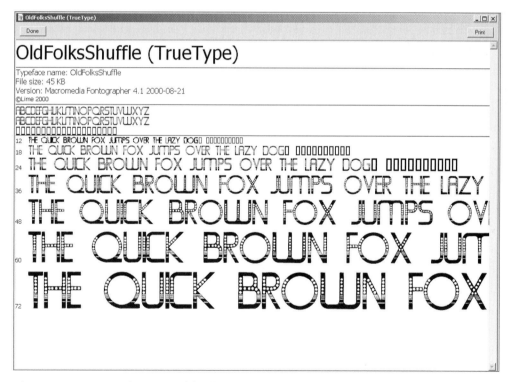

Figure 5.7 House of Lime's OldFolksShuffle font opened in its own window.

If you collect a lot of fonts, you may find it helpful to use a font manager. There are some excellent freeware font utilities, including The Font Thing, as well as commercial font management applications such as Suitcase from Extensis, which allows you to organize fonts into categories and quickly install and uninstall them.

Adding Basic Text

You don't have to use an image editor to add text to a layout. You may find it easier to use a word processing application such as Word, or a desktop publisher like Publisher, to do text boxes to add to paper layouts. These types of applications actually have better features for developing text to add to images, so if you have a lot of journaling to add, or want to do more complex text effects, they may be better suited. However, for most common text techniques, the image editor with which you're already comfortable will do a fine job.

It's more efficient for your computer to work on smaller images, especially when working with lots of text, so it's a good idea to plan your layout first, and get an approximate idea of how large you want your text blocks and titles to appear on the finished layout. Create the text blocks as separate images if you need to use a lot of journaling, and copy and paste them into the larger layout.

NOTE

Resizing text blocks by a significant amount after they are completed probably won't give you the best result. Minor adjustments are no problem, but resizing by more than 10% either way will likely result in fuzzy or distorted text. It's important to plan out layouts in advance to leave enough space for journaling and titles, in the size appropriate to your layout design.

Use fonts of varying sizes and styles to create a graphic-style page with impact. In Figure 5.8, Samuel Kordik used Trajan Pro, English 111 Vivace BT, Times New Roman, Pristina, and Edwardian Script ITC to create a simple layout that tells the story. Samuel also added a faux perspective shadow to a couple works, but used a completely different font as the shadow.

Choose a point size that's going to be appropriate for your page—remember that it's going to look bigger if printed. Too often, digital layouts are created with journaling that overwhelms the printed page. Think about what size you might read the text in a

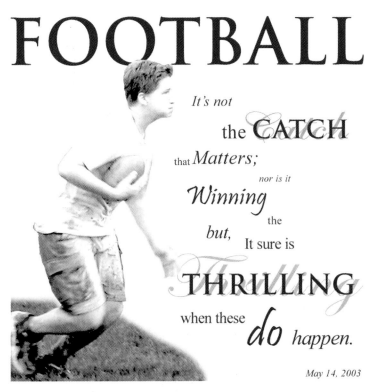

Figure 5.8 "Football" layout by Samuel Kordik.

magazine ad. Of course, if your layout is destined for a Web graphic or e-mail, you might want the text size to be larger in relation to the layout itself. Figure 5.9 shows a sample of text in Adobe Photoshop Elements 2.0.

Figure 5.9 Text in Photoshop Elements 2.0.

To add text to an image, use these steps in your image editor:

■ **Digital Image Pro 9.** From the Text menu, choose Insert Text. A text box will appear on your image, with the text entry field highlighted. Place the mouse cursor at the beginning of this field and begin typing. You can resize and reshape the text box by dragging its handles. Change the text box fill color, or choose No Fill, from the Text menu. You can edit the text properties much like you can in Word, changing the font, choosing alignment options, modifying the line spacing and indentation, adding bullets or numbering, and adding drop caps. There are several ways to modify the color of the text. Change the text color by right-clicking the text box, and choosing Font from the menu offered. You can also easily add a drop shadow to the text from that menu. Gradient fills may be added by going to Effects > Fill with Texture or Color and choosing Color, Gradient, or Pattern fills.

■ **Paint Shop Pro 8.1.** Set the Foreground and Background colors as desired, even gradients and patterns. The Foreground color will be the Stroke color and the Background color will become the Fill color; any font style can easily be used to create filled and outlined text. Activate the Text tool on the Tools toolbar. Choose the font and set the options in the Tool Options palette, including Stroke Width, if you'd like outlined text. Choose the Vector text mode to allow the most flexibility in editing the text later. Click the image and type the text you want to enter. Click OK to apply the text. You can resize and move the text using the box handles.

■ **Photoshop Elements 2.0.** Set the Foreground color as desired. Activate the Text tool, and set the text options, including vertical text, in the tool options bar. Click the image and begin typing. Use the Move tool to reposition the text.

■ **PhotoImpact XL.** Activate the Text tool. Set the text options, including color—which can be solid, gradient, or a pattern—style, size, alignment, and the Mode—which allows you to quickly create 3D text effects. Click the image and begin typing. PhotoImpact XL has amazing flexibility with text.

■ **PhotoPlus 9.** Set the Foreground color to the desired text color, and activate the Text tool. Click the image where you'd like to apply the text, and the Text Entry box will open. Set the text attributes such as font, size, and alignment. Type the desired text in the box and click OK to apply. Use the Mover tool to position the text where you like.

Some of the applications have other features that extend their text-handling capabilities. PhotoImpact XL allows you to "bend" text using the Horizontal and Vertical Deform modes of the Text tool. The colorful rainbow gradient text shown in Figure 5.10 got its shape and shadow as part of applying the text.

Other image editors have special features as well. Digital Image Pro 9 can add *drop caps* (large initials as the first letter of a text block) and wrap text around objects. Paint Shop Pro 8.1 can adjust the *kerning* (space between letters) and *leading* (space between lines of text) from within the text tool functions. In Photoshop Elements 2.0, you can apply text in a vertical orientation, and quickly add special effects using the Layer Styles palette. Just click the style of your choice, drag it to the text, and drop it, as shown in Figure 5.11.

Figure 5.10 Shaped text in PhotoImpact XL.

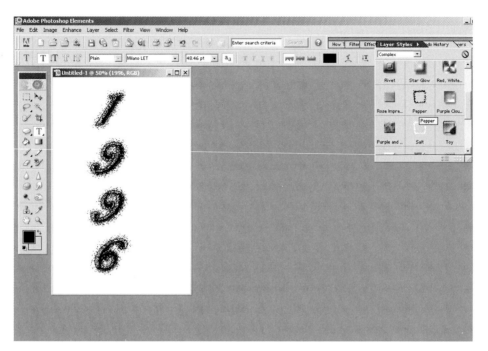

Figure 5.11 "Peppered" vertical text in Photoshop Elements 2.0.

Text elements on scrapbook layouts don't always have to conform to strict design rules, although for legibility's sake, it's a good idea to use a serif or plain font for text blocks with lots of journaling. However, you can highlight important words in a journal block by changing the font style, size, and color for those particular words. In Figure 5.12, "Ashley Turns 7 Years Old" uses diverse font styles—a legible, serif-style font for the journaling block, a decorative title font, and a fun font for the labels.

In Figure 5.13, Samuel Kordik emphasizes the sheer joy, as well as the speed and motion of sledding, by using special effects on the letters. A motion blur on the word "sledding" and a combination of glow and bevel effects on the word "extreme" all translate to a joyous small boy having the time of his life.

From sweet young lady to beautiful young lady...I cannot believe how fast you are growing up. I look at these pictures and wonder where the time goes. I love those blue eyes and bright smile. You have always been a dear daughter and I hope we will maintain a good relationship when you move on to your future. Just keep that precious heart and smile, and you will go far in life!

HAT

FIRST WATCH

NEW DRESSES

SKATE PARTY

ASHLEY TURNS 7 Years Old

Figure 5.12 "Ashley Turns 7 Years Old" by Kim Liddiard. Fonts used—CK Centurion, Engebrechtre Ink, and Embossing Tape 1 BRK.

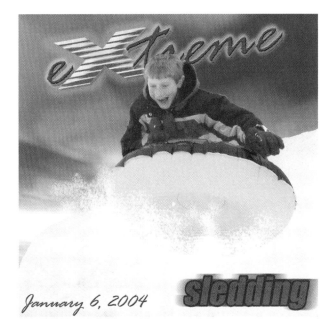

eXtreme

January 6, 2004

sledding

Figure 5.13 "Extreme Sledding" by Samuel Kordik. Fonts used—Rage Italic, Arial.

Text Selections

You can add text in a variety of colors, gradients, and patterns, with a few special effects, but in many applications it's possible to add text in other forms. Specifically, you can employ a shape selection, which can be filled with any image or used to create effects on other images. To add selection text to an image, follow these steps:

- ■ **Digital Image Pro 9.** Insert the text of your choice in a color that contrasts from the image background. Activate the Magic Wand selection tool. Uncheck Contiguous and set the selection mode to Create a New Selection. Click directly on a portion of the text. You may need to adjust the Tolerance setting to select all the text. You can delete the text itself, while retaining the selection, by clicking Delete on the keyboard, or Edit > Delete in the application.

- ■ **Paint Shop Pro 8.1.** Activate the Text tool and choose Selection from the Create as mode drop-down dialog box. Apply the text to see the selection marquee.

- ■ **Photoshop Elements 2.0.** Choose the Horizontal or Vertical Type Mask tool. This allows you to create a selection with many of the same features as the standard Type tools.

- ■ **PhotoImpact XL.** Activate the Text tool and choose Selection from the Mode drop-down dialog box.

- ■ **PhotoPlus 9.** Activate the Text Selection tool and apply the selection, just as you would do with normal text.

Creating a text-shaped selection allows you to fill letters individually, if the application you're using doesn't allow that as part of standard text creation. You can also copy the selection and use it on another image, or in the same image in a different area.

In Figure 5.14, text selections are used to cut out photo-filled text, which is then pasted in the lower-left corner of the layout. The original cutout section gets a drop shadow treatment to emphasize the depth of the cutout, and the same type of drop shadow is added to the matching photo text.

Figure 5.14 "Poppy" by Sally Beacham. Fonts used—Bickley Script, Victorian LET Plain, and Vivaldi Italic.

Vector Text Advantages

Some of the applications allow the creation of text as *vector text*. This type of text creation generally allows for more flexibility in editing the text—you can resize, recolor, and reshape the text more easily if it's in vector format. Vector text is also more easily resized; there are no pixels to produce jagged edges as the text is scaled up.

NOTE

Computer images are one of two types: raster images, which are composed of pixels, and vector images, which use geometric characteristics to describe objects. Vector graphics have certain limitations (not good for photographs), but they're good for text and line art.

Vector text can usually be made to follow curves and shapes for interesting titles. Even if an application doesn't specifically state that it has a vector text mode, it may still offer tools that allow additional editing, especially for wrapping and shaping text. PhotoImpact XL has a Wrap Gallery of shapes that can be applied to text. Photoshop Elements 2.0 has a Warp Text option that allows you to bend both vertical and horizontal text. Digital Image Pro 9 has an Insert Shaped Text option. Paint Shop Pro 8.1 has the ability to wrap text around an object or a path, as shown in Figure 5.15. The "Canada Day 2004" text follows a curved line path that is invisible in the finished layout.

Figure 5.15 "Canada Day 2004" layout by Sally Beacham. Fonts used—Bradley Hand ITC and Gill Sans MT.

Three Terrific Text Effects

Special text effects can mean the difference between an average layout and a special one. Now you'll learn how to create several popular text effects.

Transparent Vellum Text

Translucent vellum paper is a staple in paper scrapbooking, so naturally it's a popular look to re-create for a digital layout. In Figure 5.16, Delta Hey Max Nine, a font from Larabie Fonts (found on the book's resource CD), is used to create a text selection in Adobe Photoshop Elements 2.0. Create a new layer above the original photo layer, and use the Horizontal Type Mask tool to apply a text selection to that empty layer. Change to the Move tool, and open the Effects panel. Drag and drop the Text Panel effect directly on top of the text selection. Use the Move tool to resize the text block as needed. You can intensify the effect by duplicating the Text selection layer on top of the original text selection layer.

A similar effect can be achieved in Digital Image Pro 9 by applying standard text, and then lowering the Transparency (see Figure 5.17). Click the text object, go to Effects > Transparency > Even and set the Transparency to about 45. You can add a Shadow to

Figure 5.16 Vellum text effect in Photoshop Elements 2.0.

Figure 5.17 Vellum text effect in Digital Image Pro 9.

create a little depth. Go to Effects > Shadow, choose a drop shadow, and customize it to a Transparency of 35, Edge Softness of 10, and drag the shadow so that it lies close to the text itself.

Paint Shop Pro 8.1 and PhotoPlus 9 allow you to place the text on a separate layer, above your photo or image, and then lower the opacity of just that layer. Add shadows as desired, using the standard shadow tools discussed in earlier chapters.

If you're using PhotoImpact XL, apply the desired text to the image. Go to Object > Properties and adjust the transparency of the text, and then add a shadow as desired.

Photo Text

Scrapbookers love to create text headlines and titles from photos, and it couldn't be easier in the digital world. Open a photo you'd like to use for the text in your image editor, and create a text selection. This sort of effect looks best with a wide font style, so you can see the photo image inside the text. Figure 5.18 shows a text selection made on

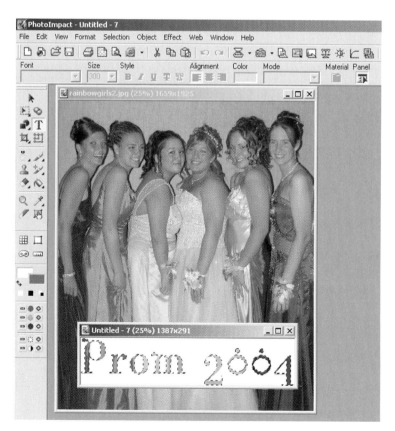

Figure 5.18 Photo text effect in PhotoImpact XL.

a photo in PhotoImpact XL, and then copied and pasted as a new image to use as a separate title.

In Figure 5.19, the title is added to a layout made from Lauren Bavin's "Color My World" page layout kit. The title font is Rina from Larabie Fonts. Mirielle, a font from Typadelic, as well as Mistral, a widely available freeware font, are used to create the faded-out background text. The layout kit, Mirielle, and Rina are available on the book's CD.

Figure 5.19 "Prom 2004" layout by Sally Beacham, elements from Lauren Bavin. Fonts used—Rina, Mirielle, and Mistral.

Shaped Text

Text that follows a shape is often used in digital scrapbook layouts. Image editors may call this feature Word Art, text on a path, or shaped text. In PhotoImpact XL, it's easy to deform text. While the Text tool is active, choose Horizontal Deform or Vertical Deform from the Mode menu of the Tool Options palette, and you can shape the text easily.

Digital Image Pro 9 allows you to choose an Insert Shaped Text option in the Text menu (see Figure 5.20). You can choose from many styles of Word Art shapes. Set the font, text color, and size after you insert the text box.

Photoshop Elements 2.0 gives you a Warp Text option right on the Type Tool options palette (see Figure 5.21). Set the text options you'd like, click the Warp Text button, and you'll be presented with a catalog of customizable shapes.

Paint Shop Pro 8.1 allows you to add text along the edges of any vector shape or path (see Figure 5.22). Create a shape using the Preset Shape tool with no fill and the stroke width set to 1. You can also use the Pen tool with similar settings to create a path. Activate the Text tool, set the options to include the Vector text mode, and hover the mouse cursor over the edge of the shape until you see the special cursor change indicating text on a path. Type in the text you'd like and click Apply. The text will magically follow the edge of the shape! You'll need to turn off the visibility of the layer that contains the vector shape or path after you apply the text if you don't want to see it in the layout.

Figure 5.23 shows a finished graphic-style layout using a shaped text headline, and three different fonts: Sylfaen, Tempus Sans ITC, and Abadi Condensed Light.

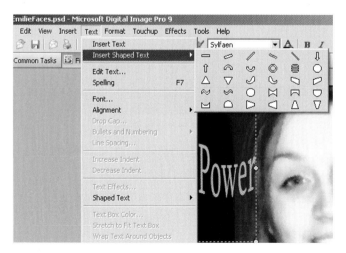

Figure 5.20 Shaped text option in Digital Image Pro 9.

Figure 5.21 Warp Text option in Photoshop Elements 2.0.

Figure 5.22 Vector text on a path in Paint Shop Pro 8.1.

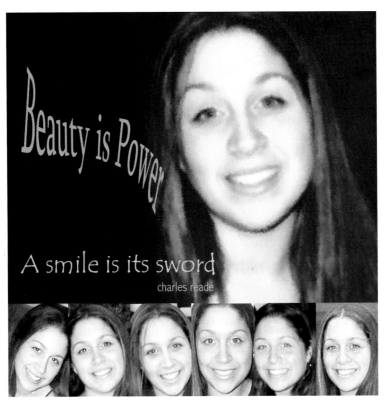

Figure 5.23 "Beauty is Power" layout by Sally Beacham.

Using Premade Alphabets

Many digital scrapbook designers create special alphabets from pre-existing fonts. Some of these come with extensive character sets, but generally you'll see just uppercase and lowercase letters, numbers, punctuation, and a few symbols.

On the book's CD, you'll find premade alphabets from Lauren Bavin, Tracy Pori, Maya, and Jenna Robertson. Premade alphabets come in two types. One type has a single multilayered image with all the letters and symbols in the image. Open the image in your application of choice. Select the letter you want, copy it, and then paste it into the layout image as desired. Continue to select, copy, and paste the remaining letters until you've created your title.

Premade alphabets are also presented in a multiple-image format. Each letter or symbol is a single image. It's easiest to open the application browser, choose the letters you want, open them all in the application, and then copy/paste them into the layout. In Figure 5.24, Tracy Pori's Circus kit and alphabet from the book's CD are used to create the title, paper mats, and photo corners.

You can colorize and resize premade alphabets just as you would any other digital scrapbook element, giving you countless options from a single alphabet set.

Figure 5.24 "Makayla" layout by Sally Beacham. Page kit and alphabet by Tracy Pori.

Mom and *Stephanie*
Summer 1997

6

Enhancing Your Pages with Filters

You've been working with photos and layouts in the image editor of your choice to this point, but now we'd like to introduce you to some exciting software options that can save you time as well as help you create stunning effects. Figure 6.1 shows a layout from Lauren Bavin. Some of the pieces in the layout kit included on the CD were produced with the help of a plug-in from Auto FX Software.

Filters, Plug-ins, and Effects

You may see the terms *filters*, *effects*, *plug-ins*, or *plug-in filters* used in conjunction with image editing applications. These terms can be interchangeable. Technically, the term *filter* refers to an image effect that emulates a photographic effect produced by an add-on camera filter. *Effects* are generally considered to be features native to an image editor. An example of a native effect is the Drop Shadow effect in Paint Shop Pro 8.1.

Defining Filters and Plug-ins

Plug-in filters are separate applications, which use the image editor as a *host*. These filters are sometimes referred to as *third-party plug-ins*, meaning another company has developed them for use with the host application. There are a few plug-ins that can be used as standalone applications as well. The Auto FX and Virtual Painter plug-ins included on the CD are examples of dual-use plug-in applications.

Figure 6.1 "Time Flies" layout by Lauren Bavin. Plug-ins used—Auto FX DreamSuite Series One.

You may also see plug-ins referred to as simply *filters*. The term *plug-ins* is commonly used to describe commercial plug-in applications, and the term *filters* to describe freeware or shareware plug-in applications. Either term is correct—they all bring cool stuff to our layouts! Figure 6.2 shows a layout by Sandi Ducote. It uses Auto FX's Photo/Graphic Edges 6.0 to produce the edge effects on the photo, which she has combined with a premade layout kit by Kim Liddiard of www.thedigitalscrapbookplace.com.

Most plug-in filters are also referred to as Photoshop-compatible plug-ins. This means that the plug-in is created to work with *any* image host that conforms to Adobe Photoshop plug-in standards. All of the image editors discussed in this book comply to one degree or another. Adobe Photoshop Elements is the most compliant, and Digital Image Pro is the least compliant. Please check for specific image host compatibility with the plug-in manufacturer before purchasing any plug-in to be sure it will work with the host you're using.

Figure 6.2 "Port Aransas" layout by Sandi Ducote. Layout kit by Margie Lundy. Plug-in used—Auto FX Photo/Graphic Edges 6.0.

NOTE

Certain native effects and filters from some applications can be made to work in other host applications. For example, most of the native filters from Photoshop 5 and 5.5 can be made to work in Paint Shop Pro and PhotoImpact. However, the filters from later versions of Photoshop won't work in other image editors due to changes in the programming of Photoshop. PhotoImpact's Art Texture plug-in will work in Paint Shop Pro. The Impressionist plug-in, which was included in Image Composer, the image editor included with some versions of Microsoft's FrontPage 98, will also work in other image editors.

In other cases, third-party plug-ins will work in host applications only if they're installed first to Photoshop, or in some cases to Corel's PhotoPaint. The Extensis line of plug-ins is a good example of this type of plug-in.

Plug-in filters can create effects in various categories. Some of those categories are:

- **Color correction and enhancement.** Auto FX's Mystical Tint Tone and Color is a good example as is The Plugin Site's ColorWasher plug-in.
- **Lighting effects.** Auto FX's Mystical Lighting, Andromeda's Shadow, and Alien Skin's Eye Candy 4000 Shadow Lab.
- **Bevel and metallic effects.** Alien Skin's Eye Candy 4000 Bevel Boss, Flaming Pear's Super BladePro, and Auto FX's DreamSuite Liquid Metal, Metal Mixer, and Dimension X.
- **Texture effects.** Auto FX's DreamSuite, The Plugin Site's HyperTyle, Namesuppressed's Plaid Lite, and Redfield Plugin's Jama 3D and Lattice Composer.
- **Sharpening and focus correction.** The Plugin Site's FocalBlade and nik's Sharpener Pro.
- **Natural and particle effects.** Alien Skin's Xenofex 2 Lightning and Little Puffy Clouds, and Corel's KPT Effects.
- **Special effects.** AV Bros. Puzzle Pro 2.0 and Page Curl 2.0, Auto FX's DreamSuite Series Two, Alien Skin Xenofex 2 Television, and AmphiSoft Raster Master.
- **Edge and Frame effects.** Auto FX Photo/Graphic Edges 6.0 and Alien Skin Splat!

Native Effects in Popular Applications

All of the example image editors have built-in features that can easily create special image effects. These can usually be found in menus with names like "Effects" or "Filter". Effects of special interest to digital scrapbookers simulate paint techniques, such as watercolor or charcoal. Photos can be turned into paintings that can then be used as backgrounds or as focal point photos themselves. Figure 6.3 shows the Underpainting filter from Photoshop Elements 2.0 applied to a photo. Go to Filter > Artistic > Underpainting to find this effect.

As with many effects filters, Underpainting is customizable. There are "before and after" views in the panes at the top of the dialog box, as well as Zoom controls (the plus and minus keys). You can modify the size and coverage of the virtual brush and paint, and change the type of texture that is used to simulate the paint effect. In Figure 6.3, you see a Canvas effect, but you can also use Burlap, Brick, and Sandstone as well as custom textures of your own choice.

Figure 6.3 Photoshop Elements 2.0 Underpainting filter.

PhotoImpact XL has an interesting effect at Effect > Artistic > Kaleidoscope. This filter creates a pattern using a customizable selection from an open image, repeating and rotating the selection over the entire original image, as shown in Figure 6.4.

Digital Image Pro 9 has an Effects browser that allows you to preview all its artistic effects before you actually apply them. Go to Effects > Filters > All Filters to open the dialog. Select an effect from the list on the left, and see it previewed in the panel on the right. If you would like, you can preview certain types of effects only. Change the Filter category at the top of the panel, and you'll only see the effects of that type in the preview list. In Figure 6.5, the Pencil: Soft Sketch effect is applied to the photograph.

Figure 6.6 shows the Stained Glass effect in PhotoPlus 9. Go to Effects > Other > Stained Glass to access this dialog box. The cell size—the size of the glass "pieces"—as well as the border thickness—the "leading" between the glass pieces—are customizable.

Figure 6.4 PhotoImpact XL's Kaleidoscope filter.

Figure 6.5 Digital Image Pro 9's Pencil: Soft Sketch effect.

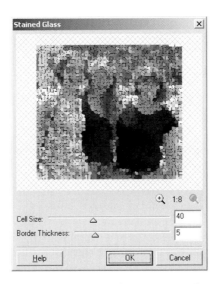

Figure 6.6 PhotoPlus 9's Stained Glass effect.

A popular image effect that's found new life in scrapbooking is the Page Curl effect. Applied to a photo or mat, this effect creates a curled edge that resembles a book page ready to be turned, often revealing another page or photo beneath. Paint Shop Pro 8.1 has a Page Curl effect built in—go to Effects > Image Effects > Page Curl to view the dialog box. Figure 6.7 shows the Page Curl dialog box, with a corner curled and a transparent area under the curl. The color of the curl, as well as the placement and radius, are customizable within the dialog box.

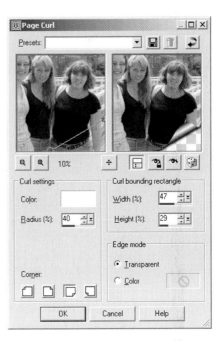

Figure 6.7 Paint Shop Pro 8.1's Page Curl effect.

TIP

To use the transparency setting in the Page Curl dialog box, the image must be on a true layer, not a background layer.

As you can see, it's possible to add interesting effects to your photos and scrapbook elements using native features of the programs without adding anything else. However, there are lots of effects that can be produced better and faster, or with more features, by using a plug-in filter.

Obtaining Plug-ins

We've already mentioned that plug-ins come in freeware, shareware, and commercial versions. Some companies produce freeware versions of a plug-in, and then a more advanced version with additional features that they market commercially. Some programmers write freeware plug-ins for the graphics community, asking nothing in return. Occasionally, plug-ins are *shareware*—free to test out and use, but if you like it and want to continue using it, the developer requests compensation.

Most commercial plug-ins have more extensive feature sets than do freeware, but not always. They often include additional resources such as texture packs and light tiles, and usually have distinctive interfaces, which may not be an advantage if you don't like playing "hide and seek" with familiar commands.

Many plug-ins make use of a handy feature called *presets*. Presets are saved settings combinations, which when loaded into the plug-in reproduce an effect previously constructed. For example, if you create a blue, chrome metallic effect in Eye Candy 4000 Chrome, you can save the settings that created it as a preset, and load it again any time in the future to quickly re-create the same effect. Exchanging presets with other users of the same plug-in can be highly addictive. For example, the users of SuperBladePro by Flaming Pear Software have entire online communities devoted to the making and exchanging of presets.

What types of effects can you create with plug-ins? Any type you can conceive and a few more! Bear in mind, if you have the knowledge, time, and patience, it's still possible to create those effects in the host image editor itself. Plug-ins sometimes add functionality to an image editor, but most often, they provide shortcuts to effects that could be created manually, if somewhat laboriously.

On this book's resource CD, you'll find many plug-in filter demo versions to try out. A word about demo versions—they come in several types, some of which are easier to work with than others. Demo versions are supplied to allow you to test-drive the plug-ins. You can test the quality of the effects as well as the functionality of the interface before you commit to a purchase.

Demo version types that you'll find on the resource CD are:

- **Time-limited, fully functional.** Alien Skin's Xenofex 2 is fully functional for 30 days. Alien Skin's Splat! is fully functional except for the Picture Tube import/export feature.

- **Fuctionality-limited, but doesn't time out.** In Eye Candy 4000, three of the 23 filters are fully functional: Glass, Marble, and Shadowlab. The other 20 filters allow you to preview, but not apply or save their effects.

- **Functional, but watermarks on finished image.** AV Bros. Page Curl and Puzzle Pro apply a watermark to images saved with the demo versions. Virtual Painter allows you to save the first 32 produced images with a small watermark, while additional images will include a larger watermark.

- **Limits function to built-in images.** Auto FX plug-ins don't allow the use of your own images in the demo version. You can use all the functions of the plug-in, but must use the images provided with the demo versions.

Several of the plug-ins on the CD are freeware plug-ins with some commercial demos as well. In particular, Redfield Plugins and AmphiSoft offer some nice effects for free.

Freeware Plug-ins

Do an Internet search for "freeware" and "plug-ins" and you'll find hundreds of links. However, there are a couple portal sites that have already done the work for you and make it easy to find some excellent freeware as well as commercial plug-ins. We recommend the following sites:

- **The Plugin Site.** www.thepluginsite.com contains links to their own plug-ins, but also reviews and links in the Reviews section. There are also many more links for both free and commercial plug-ins in the Resources section.

- **FreePhotoshop.com.** www.freephotoshop.com has hundreds of reviews and links, for both free and commercial plug-ins as well as other useful resources.

- **Graphicsoft at About.com.** http://graphicssoft.about.com/od/ pluginsfiltersfree/— lots of links to plug-ins, tutorials, and resources.

Commercial Plug-ins

There are thousands of commercial plug-ins available. Some are inexpensive (AmphiSoft, Redfield Plugins, and Namesuppressed all offer great plug-ins at a low price) and some cost more than the image editor you're using. We recommend trying demo versions of any commercial plug-in before you buy. You should make sure it will work properly with your image editor (contact the manufacturer if you are unsure) and that the plug-in creates effects you'll actually use.

Commercial plug-ins often come with extensive documentation, both built-in Help files, PDF manuals on the installation CD or available for download, and sometimes even paper manuals. This documentation can be invaluable as you'll soon discover the wide variety of interfaces and program language can make finding familiar commands and features a real treasure hunt.

Installing and Managing Plug-ins

Plug-ins can be installed just as you would install any other application, either from a CD or from a download, if you purchase online. Follow the manufacturer's instruction for installation. It's a good idea to organize how you'll install plug-ins before you start doing it. Since collecting plug-ins is just as addictive as collecting scrapbook elements, you could soon find yourself with a ton of software. If you would like to use the filters in more than one host application, or if you want to limit the amount of uninstalling and reinstalling you might have to do in the future, it's a good idea to use a single plug-ins folder that is *not* contained within the Programs folder of an image editor. That way, if you have to uninstall the host application, or if you choose to upgrade the host, you won't have to reinstall the plug-ins. Putting a folder in My Documents is a good idea. You can then set up subfolders inside that main plug-ins folder to organize plug-ins from various developers.

Some plug-ins will automatically detect a host application and try to install to that application's Program folder. You can override this by choosing a custom installation, or clicking on the Browse button to change the installation folder.

Occasionally, you'll find that a plug-in doesn't work or work properly within the host image. If you receive an error message that the plug-in isn't correctly configured, the most common cause is a corrupt version of a necessary DLL file. The simple solution is to download and install the correct version, which can be found at www.dizteq.com/joestuff/freestuff.html. You may need to install the DLL to the Windows > System folder, the Windows > System 32 folder, or the program folder of the image editor you're using. If in doubt, install it in all three.

Once you have a plug-in installed, you need to tell your image editor where to find it:

■ **Digital Image Pro 9.** Go to Tools > Options > Supplemental Software Options. Click Plug-in Filters options, and browse to the Plug-ins folder. Click OK. The plug-in filters can now be accessed by going to Effects > Plug-in Filters. A dialog will open showing all the plug-ins you have installed, as shown in Figure 6.8. Click the plug-in you would like to use, and the Launch plug-in filter command. Then, you'll enter the plug-in interface.

Figure 6.8 Digital Image Pro 9, Plug-ins Filter dialog.

- **Paint Shop Pro 8.1.** Go to File > Preferences > File Locations. In the File Types pane, click Plug-ins. In the right panel, click the Add button to add a new folder location, and then the Browse button to browse to the plug-ins folder you'll use. You can have as many plug-ins folders as you like, so if you find that one folder creates a plug-ins menu that is too long, or you don't want to load all the plug-ins all of the time, you can configure the folder path in this Preference setting quickly. To access the plug-ins, go to Effects > Plugins. Click the menu entry for the plug-in and the plug-in interface will open.

- **PhotoImpact XL.** Go to File > Preferences > General. Click the Plug-ins category, and then define up to nine separate plug-ins folder locations. If you check the box to the right of the plug-ins path, the folder will be enabled so that the filters in that folder will show up in the Plugins menu. Once the folder is enabled, go to the Effect menu, and the plug-in names will appear at the bottom of the menu. Click the plug-in name and the interface will open.

- **PhotoPlus 9.** Go to File > Preferences > Plugins tab. Click the Browse button and choose the Plugins folder. You may only have one main Plugins folder in this image editor. Once the folder is enabled, go to Effects > Plugin Filters and click the plug-in name. The interface will open.

- **Photoshop Elements 2.0.** Go to File > Edit > Preferences > Plug-ins and Scratch Disks. Check the box to enable Additional plug-ins directory, click the Choose button and browse to the Plugins folder. You may use the Plugins folder inside the Program folder for Photoshop Elements 2.0 as well as this additional folder. Go to the Filter menu, and the plug-in names will appear at the bottom of the list. Click the plug-in name and the interface will open.

Examples of Popular Plug-ins

We'll take a look at some of the plug-ins on the CD now, which cover a broad range of effects as well as prices.

Alien Skin Plug-ins

Alien Skin Software, www.alienskin.com, makes some of the best plug-ins for digital scrapbookers. Alien Skin plug-ins come with an actual paper manual to guide you as well as many presets to get you started with effects:

- **Eye Candy 4000.** Suite of 23 filter effects, including Glass, Chrome, Fire, Fur, Smoke, and Drip and Bevel Boss.
- **Eye Candy 5 Textures.** Ten filter effects, including updated versions of some of the filter effects from Eye Candy 4000 (Animal Fur, Marble, Swirl, Texture Noise, Weave, and Wood) and four new filters (Brick Wall, Diamond Plate, Reptile Skin, and Stone Wall).
- **Xenofex 2.** Fourteen filter effects, including Lightning, Constellation, Rip Open, and Flag. Some filters are particularly good for scrapbooking, including Stain, Cracks, Crumple, and Burnt Edges.
- **Splat!.** Very good for scrapbookers—effects include Fill and Border Stamp (which use Paint Shop Pro Picture Tubes) as well as Patchwork, Resurface, Edges, and Frames. Figure 6.9 shows a layout that uses Splat! as well as Eye Candy 4000 for some of its image effects.

The Alien Skin line of plug-ins use a similar interface, which is compact and easily navigated. Figure 6.10 shows the interface for the Edges filter in Splat! You can access all the filters in the plug-in suite from inside the plug-in interface, which is convenient. If you don't like one filter's effects, you can just try another one without exiting the plug-in and re-access it from the host application.

Xenofex 2 and Splat! feature some filter effects that are "most-wanted" by digital scrapbookers. Xenofex 2 can simulate crumpled paper effects and torn, burned, ripped edges. Splat! has numerous edge and frame effects that are simple to use and customize. Figure 6.11 shows an example of Crumple applied to a flower photo.

Figure 6.9 "I Love Food" layout by Samuel Kordik. Plug-ins used—Eye Candy 4000 and Splat! from Alien Skin.

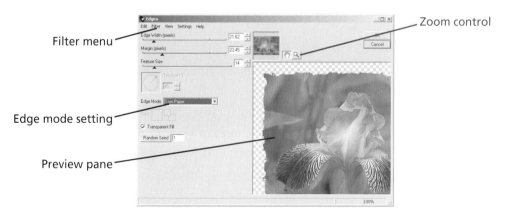

Figure 6.10 Alien Skin's Splat! Plug-in, Edges filter interface.

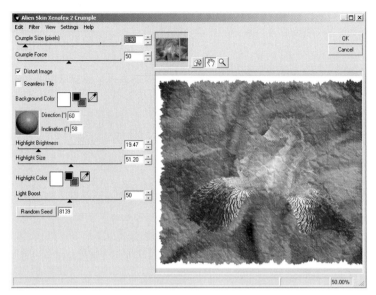

Figure 6.11 Alien Skin's Xenofex 2, Crumple filter.

The Plugin Site

ColorWasher is a color correction and enhancement plug-in from The Plugin Site at www.thepluginsite.com. This company produces great plug-ins at a reasonable cost. Some other plug-ins available from The Plugin Site include FocalBlade, a sharpening plug-in for digital photos; HyperTyle, a texture-making plug-in; Plugin Galaxy, a collection of image effects; and Harry's Filters, a freeware collection.

Figure 6.12 shows the ColorWasher interface, with a photo open that needs some correction to produce realistic white areas. The interface is shown in Easy mode, which gives the user several automatic opens for correcting the open image. If more detailed modifications are needed, the Expert mode can be accessed, which allows for more specific correction.

The resource CD for this book contains demo versions of ColorWasher, FocalBlade, and Edge and Frame Galaxy. Edge and Frame Galaxy is not a plug-in, but rather a collection of masks and edge effects that scrapbookers will find useful. For help applying mask effects, refer to your image editor's Help files and manual.

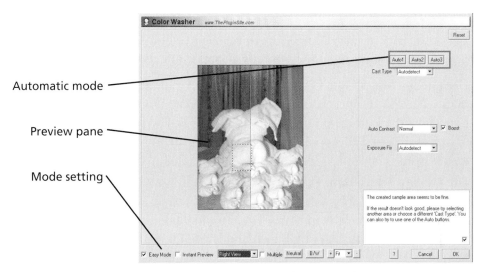

Figure 6.12 ColorWasher from The Plugin Site.

Auto FX Software

Auto FX Software, www.autofx.com, produces high-quality and somewhat expensive plug-ins (see Figure 6.13). These plug-ins share a common interface, so once you get past the hurdle of learning one plug-in suite, you're assured of navigating the rest easily. The effects produced by these plug-ins are ideally suited to digital scrapbooking, so while they may represent a healthy investment, you'll use the effects constantly.

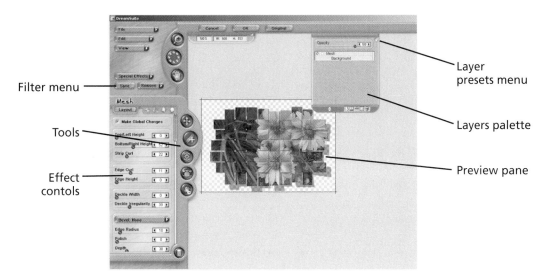

Figure 6.13 DreamSuite Series Two Mesh filter from Auto FX.

The Auto FX plug-ins also function as standalone applications. If you choose to use an image editor that doesn't use Photoshop-compatible plug-ins, you can still make use of the effects. These plug-ins include hundreds of preset effects:

- **DreamSuite Series One.** Eighteen filter effects including 35mm Frame, Insta-matic, and Photo Border for realistic edge effects. Deckle, Ripple, Crease, and Crackle add texture and dimension to photos and scrapbook elements. Metal Mixer and Liquid Metal can produce some of the most beautiful metallic effects ever.

- **DreamSuite Series Two.** Fourteen filters including $2\frac{1}{4}$ Film Frame, 4×5 Film Frame, Film Strip, Film Frame Art, and PhotoStrips. Wrinkle, PhotoPress, and Plastic Wrap add dimension, and Tile, Puzzle Pieces, and Mesh create realistic hand-crafted effects. Dreamy Photo and Mosaic are included in this suite, and are also available as freeware effects. Check out the book's resource CD for instructions on how to obtain these two filters.

- **DreamSuite Gel Series.** Five filters to create luminous and translucent gel-like painted effects.

- **Mystical Lighting.** Sixteen filters to lighting and shadow effects, some realistic, some fantastic.

- **Mystical Tint Tone and Color.** Thirty-eight filters to correct and enhance colors. There are softening effects, posterize, exposure and contrast effects as well as gradient tinting and sepia. Figure 6.14 shows a layout that uses Mystical Tint Tone and Color to modify the photo.

- **Photo/Graphic Edges 6.0.** Fourteen filters with multiple presets to create montages, frame effects, etched and burned edges, photo tabs and borders, smudged edges, and vignettes. Hundreds of presets, textures, and light tiles included.

Figure 6.14 "Santa Jeremy" layout by Sandi Ducote, from a layout kit by Kim Liddiard. Plug-in used—Auto FX Mystical Tint Tone and Color.

Other Plug-ins on the CD

On the resource CD, you'll also find plug-ins from AmphiSoft, AV Bros., NameSuppressed, Redfield Plugins, and Virtual Painter:

- **AmphiSoft Plug-in Filters.** Ten freeware and shareware filter effects. Simplifier is an easy-to-use filter that simulates paint effects. For US$18.85, this is the most value-priced filter pack you'll find anywhere.

- **AV Bros.** Puzzle Pro 2.0 and Page Curl 2.0 have the most sophisticated page curl and puzzle effects possible. Included on the CD is the freeware Colorist plug-in.

- **NameSuppressed.** Autochromatic and Softener plug-ins create color and soft focus effects. The Plaid Lite plug-in creates plaid pattern tiles from any image.

- **Redfield Plugins.** Jama 3D and Lattice Composer are superb freeware plug-ins that create realistic textures like corrugated cardboard and mesh. The commercial versions add more features and the ability to create all sorts of realistic textures.

- **Virtual Painter.** Easy-to-use paint effects plug-in. You can choose from 16 different paint effects, including Watercolor, Pastel, and Gouache, and 12 material types, including Paper, Canvas, Wood, and Cork.

Extended Examples

Plug-in filter effects can quickly produce stunning layouts with few other elements needed. In Figure 6.15, Lauren Bavin used an Auto FX Dreamy Photo effect with Photo Border effects and a couple font styles to create this simple, but effective layout.

Figure 6.15 "Sweet Child of Mine" layout by Lauren Bavin. Plugins used—Auto FX Dreamy Photo and Photo Border.

Text Effect with Eye Candy 4000

Eye Candy 4000 has superb image effects, but none as famous or useful as its metallic Chrome effect. It works particularly well on text. In Figure 6.16, Angela Cable's "Wedding" layout kit from the resource CD is used to create a page, and Eye Candy 4000 Chrome for the metallic text on the tag. The chalked effect around the letters is done with Eye Candy 4000 Corona, and the shadows added with Eye Candy 4000 Shadowlab.

Figure 6.16 "Renee & Jason" layout by Sally Beacham. Page layout kit by Angela Cable. Plug-ins used—Eye Candy 4000 Chrome, Corona, and Shadowlab.

Figure 6.17 "MHS Football 2004" layout by Sally Beacham. "Denim Dude" layout kit by Lauren Bavin. Plug-ins used—Auto FX Dreamy Photo and Mosaic.

Image Effect with Auto FX Plug-ins

The layout in Figure 6.17 is created by filtering the photos with Auto FX's Dreamy Photo and Mosaic plug-ins, both of which are freeware and are included in the Dream-Suite Series Two collection. They were layered over elements from Lauren Bavin's Denim Dude kit, available on the resource CD. The background paper and mesh is colorized to better match the photos. The wooden plank tag title is created by cutting out a text selection and adding drop shadows for depth.

Edge Effect with Splat!

Splat! from Alien Skin is an affordable plug-in with lots of effects useful to the digital scrapbooker. In Figure 6.18, the Resurface filter is used to create a canvas texture with the flower photo, which is then used as the background as well as focal point photo for the layout. The background layer is duplicated, and the duplicate layer is changed to grayscale. The portion of the duplicate layer to show in color is erased, allowing the bottom colored layer to show through. A white border is added, and then the Splat! Frame filter is used to add a decorative Dover edge. The same edge is used on the simple journal box. This layout was created in minutes with nothing but a single photo, the plug-in, and two fonts.

Figure 6.18 "Backyard Blooms" layout by Sally Beacham. Photo by Ron Lacey. Plug-ins used—Splat! Resurface and Frame filters.

Advanced Photo Techniques

In this chapter, we'll look at a few advanced photo enhancement methods. We'll begin with a method for better cropping, and then go on to a few manual methods for correcting brightness/contrast and color. We'll wrap up with some methods for converting color photos to black and white.

Better Cropping: The Rule of Thirds

In Chapter 2, "Digital Photo Fundamentals," you saw how cropping can be used to make more interesting compositions. When you look at a photo with an eye to improving its composition with cropping, try using a technique that goes back to ancient times: the Rule of Thirds.

To use the Rule of Thirds as a guide, you divide your photo into thirds both horizontally and vertically. In your composition, you want to have a strong element of your image at one of the points at which these dividing lines intersect.

NOTE

Digital Image Pro 9 has Rule of Thirds guides built right into the Crop tool.

For image editors that don't include Rule of Thirds guides, you can easily make your own. Open a new image with a transparent background. Be sure the dimensions of the image are evenly divisible by three (300 × 300 pixels, for example). Select the entire image, and then contract the selection by one and invert the selection. Paint the selection with a bright color. Turn off the selection and then draw straight lines to divide the image into thirds both horizontally and vertically. The result should look something like Figure 7.1 (where the checkerboard pattern isn't part of the image, but simply an indication of transparency).

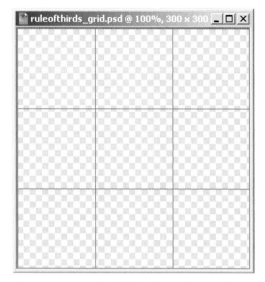

Figure 7.1 Rule of Thirds guide: made with lines dividing the image into thirds, horizontally and vertically.

Save the image in a file format that supports transparency, such as your image editor's native file format or PSD.

When you want to use your Rule of Thirds guide, open it and the photo that you want to crop. Copy the Rule of Thirds guide and paste it into the photo as a new layer. (You can then close the Rule of Thirds guide file.) The result will look something like Figure 7.2.

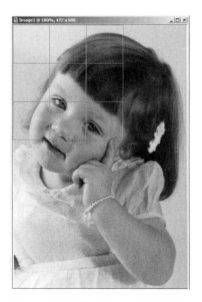

Figure 7.2 The Rule of Thirds guide pasted in as a new layer.

Use your image editor's Deform or Transform tool to resize and reposition the pasted-in guide. Try to find a composition that you like where a strong element of the photo is at one of the intersection points of the guidelines, as shown in Figure 7.3.

When you have a composition you like, use your crop tool to crop around the outer boundary of the guide (see Figure 7.4). Then delete the layer that contains the guide, and you'll have your cropped composition, as shown in Figure 7.5.

Figure 7.3 Finding the right composition.

Figure 7.4 Crop around the guide boundary.

Figure 7.5 The cropped photo.

TIP

When using the Rule of Thirds to help in creating interesting compositions, you don't have to have a point of interest at one of the points of intersection. Instead, you can use the guidelines themselves to line up important horizontal or vertical elements. For example, in a landscape set the horizon line along one of the Rule of Thirds horizontal guidelines.

Improving Brightness and Contrast

Your image editor's automatic brightness and contrast adjustment commands might be all you'll ever need for improving your photos. However, as you become more familiar with your image editor—and more particular about your photos—you'll undoubtedly want to look into the more specialized tools for controlling contrast and brightness. There are two types of brightness and contrast enhancing tools you may want to explore: Levels and Curves.

Levels

The first advanced brightness and contrast enhancer to try out is one typically called Levels (or Level). In most image editors, this command shows you a *histogram*, a graphical representation of the areas of dark and light in your image. Figure 7.6 shows PhotoImpact's Level dialog box. The histogram is the graph below the preview windows.

The left side of the histogram shows the shadows (the dark areas of the photo), the right side shows the highlights (the light areas), and the middle shows the midtones (the areas with brightness levels in between very dark and very light). The height of the graph at different points shows the amount of image data that occurs in the particular photo at different brightness levels.

Figure 7.6 The histogram shows your image's areas of light and dark.

Notice that the histogram in Figure 7.6 has no data at the extreme left side and much on the right side. This indicates that the darkest shadows contain no true black and the highlights contain no true white. The contrast of the image being edited would be improved if its histogram were adjusted so that the darkest pixels are made black (or nearly black) and the lightest pixels are made white (or nearly white). You make these adjustments by moving the triangular slider controls on the left and right below the histogram:

- To darken the shadows, drag the left slider to the area where the left end of the histogram begins.
- To lighten the highlights, drag the right slider to the area where the right end of the histogram begins.
- To adjust the overall brightness of your photo, adjust the middle slider. Moving this control over to the left brightens the image, and moving it to the right darkens the image.

In Figure 7.6, the left slider is positioned just to the point where it touches the leftmost end of the histogram, and the right slider is positioned almost to the starting point of the rightmost end of the histogram. The result is darker shadows and whiter highlights.

CAUTION

Be conservative in making the left and right slider adjustments. Go too far to the right with the left slider and you'll lose detail at the shadow end. Go too far to the left with the right slider and you'll lose detail at the highlight end.

Here's where you'll find the Levels command in some popular image editors:

Digital Image Pro 9

Touchup > Adjust Levels

Paint Shop Pro 8.1

Adjust > Brightness and Contrast > Levels

PhotoImpact XL

Format > Level

PhotoPlus 9

Image > Adjust > Levels

Photoshop Elements 2.0

Enhance > Adjust Brightness/Contrast > Levels

NOTE

Paint Shop Pro's Levels command doesn't feature a histogram. For a command more like the Levels command in other image editors, Paint Shop Pro users should try Adjust > Brightness and Contrast > Histogram Adjustment instead.

Curves

Another brightness and contrast enhancement command is Curves (called Tone Map in PhotoImpact). This command is quite powerful and may not be available in your image editor. For example, although Photoshop has a Curves command, Photoshop Elements 2.0 doesn't. Digital Image Pro 9 also doesn't include Curves.

Curves allows you to fine-tune brightness and contrast along the whole tonal range, from shadows to highlights, adjusting any number of subranges. To see how, take a look at Figure 7.7, which shows the Curves dialog box in Paint Shop Pro 8.1. The most prominent element in the dialog box is a graph that represents the modified and original brightness values of your image.

Figure 7.7 Curves features a graph of brightness values.

The graph in Figure 7.7 represents the input and output brightness values along the whole tonal range, with shadows represented at the left side and highlights on the right, with black at the bottom and white at the top. When you open Curves, the graph is a straight line from the lower left to the upper right because the input and output values match up 1-to-1 before you make any adjustments.

You make adjustments by dragging any node on the curve. When you begin, there are only two nodes, one at the far left (for black) and one at the far right (for white). To add new nodes along the curve, just click on the curve. To lighten pixels at any point, click a node and drag upward. To darken pixels at any point, click a node and drag downward. Figures 7.8 and 7.9 show examples of each.

You can even produce a negative version of your photo with Curves. Just drag the leftmost node to the top and the rightmost node to the bottom, completely inverting the original curve. An example is shown in Figure 7.10.

Contrast in any area is affected by the steepness of the graph in that area. The steeper the curve, the higher the contrast. Figures 7.11 and 7.12 show examples of increasing the contrast.

Figure 7.8 Lightening areas of an image with Curves.

Figure 7.9 Darkening areas of an image with Curves.

Figure 7.10 Creating a negative version with Curves.

Figure 7.11 Increasing the contrast in an area by increasing the graph's steepness.

Figure 7.12 Increasing contrast even further.

A common rule of thumb is that a photo benefits by having a slightly S-shaped curve, as shown in Figure 7.13.

There are many exceptions to this rule, so don't be a slave to it. Keep in mind that what this curve does is increase the contrast for the midtones by sacrificing detail in the shadow and highlight ranges. One situation in which an S-shaped curve would be particularly inappropriate is where the photo already has high contrast.

CAUTION

One problem with Curves is that it can produce unintended changes to your image's color. To avoid this problem, try the following technique:

1. Duplicate the Background layer of your photo.

2. On the duplicate layer, apply Curves.

3. Set the blending mode of the duplicate layer to Luminance or Lightness.

4. Adjust the duplicate layer's opacity until you get the effect you want.

Figure 7.13 An S-curve can benefit many photos.

Here's where you'll find Curves in some popular image editors:

Paint Shop Pro 8.1

> Adjust > Brightness and Contrast > Curves

PhotoImpact XL

> Format > Tone Map

PhotoPlus 9

> Image > Adjust > Curves

Manual Color Adjusting

Most color photos could use a little color adjustment. Your photo may have a color cast, perhaps because it was shot with the camera's white balance set inappropriately for the lighting conditions or maybe your camera or scanner is sensitive to some colors more than others. If your image is a scan of a film photo, maybe you used the wrong film type for the lighting conditions. Whatever the case, your image editor provides you with a number of tools for correcting problems with color.

Understanding Color in Digital Images

Full-color computer images are represented as combinations of color information. There are several color models; the most common is the Red-Green-Blue (or RGB) model. In this model, all colors are represented as combinations of red, green, and blue. For example, in this method equal amounts of red and green make yellow, while equal amounts of green and blue make cyan and equal amounts of blue and red make magenta. If the amount of all three color "channels"—red, green, and blue—are equal, the result is neutral gray.

There are 256 levels of brightness for each of the three color channels, the lowest level is 0 and the highest is 255. If all three color channels have a value of 0, the result is black. If all three have a value of 255, the result is white. Because there are three channels each with 256 possible values, the total number of colors that can be represented is approximately 16.7 million ($256 \times 256 \times 256$).

Another way to represent color digitally is with the Hue-Saturation-Lightness (or HSL) model. Like the RGB model, the HSL model represents colors in three channels. In this model, there's one channel for hue, one for saturation, and one for lightness.

Hue is pretty much what you might normally think of as color: red, yellow, green, and so on. Saturation is the purity, intensity, or vividness of the color. A totally saturated color is the pure color, a totally unsaturated color is gray, and other saturations give results in between.

Lightness is the level of brightness in your image. Increasing the lightness makes the image brighter, and decreasing it makes it darker.

Color correcting commands in your image editor make use of one of these two color models. Some affect color balance (the relative amounts of red, green, and blue), while others affect hue or saturation.

Common Situations Requiring Color Correction

Probably the most common use for color correcting commands is to eliminate color casts. The color of the objects in your photo is affected by the color of the ambient light at the time your photo was taken. Photos taken indoors under incandescent light will have a yellowish cast. Photos taken outdoors in the shade will have a bluish cast. By adjusting the color balance, you can remove the cast. Figure 7.14 shows an example where the yellowish cast is removed by adding more blue, the opposite of yellow in the RGB color model. (The command used in the example is Paint Shop Pro's Color Balance.)

Figure 7.14 One way to eliminate a color cast.

Another common color correction task is saturation adjustment. For example, photos in which you've increased the brightness can look washed out. In this case, you'd want to increase the saturation to bring back the vividness of the colors. On the other hand, in portraits the saturation might be too high. In that case, you'd want to bring the saturation down a bit to make the colors look more natural.

Here are a few color and saturation adjustment commands available in some popular image editors:

Digital Image Pro 9

> Touchup > Hue and Saturation

Paint Shop Pro 8.1

> Adjust > Color Balance > Channel Mixer
>
> Adjust > Color Balance > Color Balance
>
> Adjust > Color Balance > Grey World Color Balance
>
> Adjust > Color Balance > Manual Color Correction
>
> Adjust > Hue and Saturation > Hue/Saturation/Lightness

PhotoImpact XL

> Format > Color Balance
>
> Format > Color Adjustment
>
> Format > Color Cast
>
> Format > Hue & Saturation

PhotoPlus 9

> Image > Adjust > Color Balance
>
> Image > Adjust > Hue/Saturation Lightness
>
> Image > Adjust > Channel Mixer

Photoshop Elements 2.0

> Enhance > Adjust Color > Color Cast
>
> Enhance > Adjust Color > Hue/Saturation
>
> Enhance > Adjust Color > Color Variations

Of these applications, Paint Shop Pro and PhotoPlus's Channel Mixer and Paint Shop Pro's Manual Color Correction are probably the most complex. If you use Paint Shop Pro or PhotoPlus, give the other color correction commands a try first before trying to tackle Channel Mixer or Manual Color Correction. The other listed commands are pretty straightforward. Consult your image editor's manual or Help file for more information.

Setting Black, White, and Gray Points

As funny as it might sound, you can correct the color in your photos by telling your image editor what parts of the photo should be black, white, or gray. By determining what part of the image should be neutral, some color correction commands can then determine how to adjust the overall colors to get the proper balance, eliminating any color cast.

Commands like these have one or more eyedroppers. You select an eyedropper, and then click on a part of the photo that should be neutral. Figure 7.15 shows an example using Digital Image Pro's Adjust Tint command, which lets you pick an area in your photo that should be pure white.

Figure 7.15 Balancing color by selecting a neutral point.

Here's a list of commands that include eyedroppers for setting black, white, or gray points:

Digital Image Pro 9

Touchup > Adjust Tint

Paint Shop Pro 8.1

Adjust > Color Balance > Black and White Points

PhotoImpact XL

Format > Level

Format > Tone Map

PhotoPlus 9

Image > Adjust > Levels

Photoshop Elements 2.0

Enhance > Adjust Brightness/Contrast > Levels

TIP

The best way to eliminate a color cast is not getting one in the first place. Be sure to consult your camera's manual to see how to adjust white balance for particular lighting situations when you're shooting your photos.

From Color to Black and White

Some digital cameras have a black and white option, enabling you to capture your photos as black and white images rather than in color. Sometimes you'll have a color photo that you'd like to convert to black and white, and you may even find that the black and white versions your camera produces don't give quite the results you want. Fortunately, it's easy to convert a color photo to black and white.

Desaturation

One of the easiest ways to go from color to black and white is to desaturate your image. Saturation is the vividness or purity of a color, ranging from totally pure to totally gray. By setting the saturation as low as it can go, you can change a color photo to black and white.

One problem with this method is all colors that have the same level of lightness, differing only in saturation and hue, will become the exact same shade of gray. Compare Figures 7.16 and 7.17, where the first is a series of colored blocks and the second is the desaturated version of that same image.

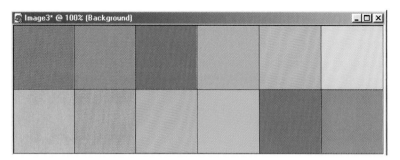

Figure 7.16 Image where all colors are of the same lightness.

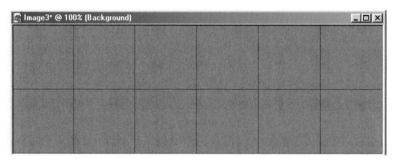

Figure 7.17 Desaturated version of the same image.

Of course, you won't find that all of the colors in any of your photographs have the exact same level of lightness, so desaturating your photos will never give you the extreme results shown in Figure 7.17. However, you're almost certain to lose at least some of the detail in your photo if you use desaturation. For some photos, the loss of detail may be barely noticeable, though, so don't rule out desaturation altogether.

Here's a list of desaturation commands in some common image editors:

Digital Image Pro 9

   Touchup > Hue and Saturation

Paint Shop Pro 8.1

   Adjust > Hue and Saturation > Colorize

   Adjust > Hue and Saturation > Hue/Saturation/Lightness

PhotoImpact XL

   Format > Hue & Saturation

PhotoPlus 9

   Image > Adjust > Hue/Saturation/Lightness

Photoshop Elements 2.0

> Enhance > Adjust Color > Remove Color
>
> Enhance > Adjust Color > Hue/Saturation

Converting to Grayscale

Another easy way to convert a color photo to black and white is to change the mode of your image from RGB to Grayscale. A grayscale image has no colors, but instead is made up of 256 shades of gray (including pure black and pure white). You'll still lose some detail because you'll be changing a photo that contains thousands or even millions of different colors into one that contains only 256 levels of gray. However, the results are better than what you get from desaturation, as shown in Figure 7.18.

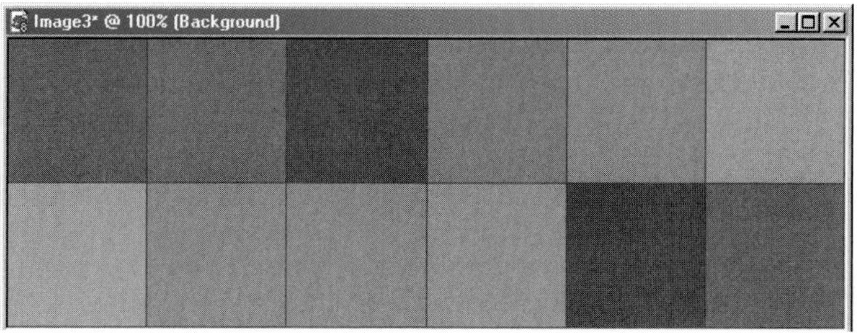

Figure 7.18 Grayscale version of Figure 7.16.

Here are the commands in several popular image editors for converting to grayscale:

Digital Image Pro 9

> Effects > Black and White

Paint Shop Pro 8.1

> Image > Greyscale

PhotoImpact XL

> Format > Data Type > Grayscale

PhotoPlus 9

> Image > Adjust > Grayscale

Photoshop Elements 2.0

> Image > Mode > Grayscale

Most of your image editor's available special effects and adjustments for color images are also available for grayscale images. Exceptions are adjustments that affect color because a grayscale image has no color. If your image editor produces true grayscale images and you want to introduce color into an image that has been converted to grayscale, you'll first need to change the image mode back to full color:

Paint Shop Pro 8.1

>Image > Increase Color Depth > 16 Million Colors (24 bit)

PhotoImpact XL

>Format > Data Type > RGB True Color

Photoshop Elements 2.0

>Image > Mode > RGB Color

This conversion back to full color is unnecessary in Digital Image Pro and PhotoPlus, where the grayscale conversion and the switch back to full-color mode is made all at once automatically.

Black and White with Channel Mixing

Only Paint Shop Pro and PhotoPlus have channel mixing commands that can be used to create black and white effects:

Paint Shop Pro 8.1

>Adjust > Color Balance > Channel Mixer

PhotoPlus 9

>Image > Adjust > Channel Mixer

Photoshop has channel mixing capabilities as well, but Photoshop Elements 2.0 does not. If by the time you're reading this you're using a later version of Digital Image Pro, PhotoImpact, or Photoshop Elements than the ones mentioned here, check to see whether channel mixing has been added.

Channel mixing for color correction can be a bit tricky, but when it comes to converting a color photo to black and white, channel mixing is not too difficult and can give some incredibly nice results.

Recall that in the RGB color model, colors are represented as three channels: one red, one blue, and one green. Each pixel in your photo has values for each of these channels, with 256 possible values for each channel, ranging from 0 to 255. Now a grayscale image has 256 shades of gray, including black (with a value of 0) and white (with a value of 255), so a channel can be represented as a grayscale image.

That might sound more than a little abstract, so let's look at an example. We'll make use of Paint Shop Pro's ability to split a color image into its separate channels. Figure 7.19 shows a full-color image, and Figures 7.20 through 7.22 show the separate color channels for that image.

Each of the channels looks like a grayscale image, but each one is different from the others. Channel mixing enables you to create a black and white version of your image that uses any one of the channels or any combination of the channels to create a black and white version of your color image. In the example photo, the green channel contains a lot of detail, the red channel shows the greatest contrast with the background, and the blue channel provides little, if any, useful information.

Figure 7.19 A color image.

Figure 7.20 The image's Red channel.

Figure 7.21 The image's Green channel.

Figure 7.22 The image's Blue channel.

Converting the photo in Figure 7.19 to grayscale gives you the result in Figure 7.23. Compare that to the version in Figure 7.24, a combination of 76% of the Red channel, 42% of the Green channel, and -18% of the Blue channel.

Figure 7.23 Grayscale version of Figure 7.19.

The channel mixing version is the more interesting image. The subject is more distinct from the background while the detail in the midtones and highlights is still maintained.

To perform channel mixing, start Channel Mixer. Choose the monochrome setting, and then adjust the percentages for each of the color channels, making sure that the percentage totals 100% if you don't want to affect the photo's overall brightness. (Total percentages higher than 100 increase brightness; total percentages less than 100 decrease brightness.) Figure 7.25 shows the Paint Shop Pro version of Channel Mixer used on a portrait.

Figure 7.24 Channel Mixer version: 76% Red, 42% Green, and -18% Blue.

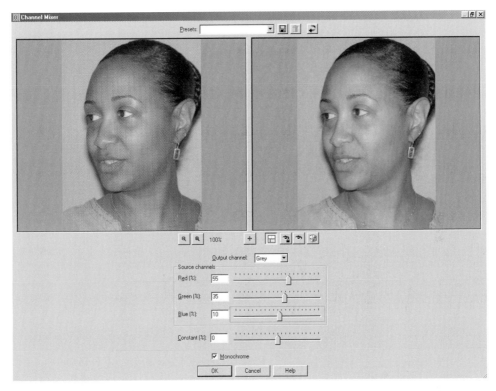

Figure 7.25 Channel Mixer in action.

TIP

In most photos, a lot of detail is contained in the Green channel. For landscapes and other photos where detail is important, maximizing the Green channel is usually ideal. For portraits, you don't want to emphasize facial blemishes, pores, and wrinkles, so in these cases keep the Green channel in check.

The Blue channel often contains quite a bit of noise. Most of the time, it's a good idea to minimize use of the Blue channel.

For example, in the portrait in Figure 7.25 good results came with settings of 55% Red, 35% Green, and 10% Blue.

Variations on Black and White

Before leaving this chapter, let's look at a few variations on black and white that can provide something extra in your layouts. We'll begin with simple tinting, then look at other kinds of colorizing, and end with a nice effect where a photo frames itself.

Tinted Black and White

Normal black and white is great for many layouts, but sometimes you'll want something just a little different. Maybe you want to simulate the old-fashioned look of sepia, or maybe you just want a monochromatic color version of your photo. You can get either of these effects by tinting your photo.

Some tinting commands let you directly tint your color photo without first converting it to black and white. That's usually fine, but in some cases you might get better results by converting to black and white first. Doing so also allows you to improve the brightness and contrast of your untinted black and white version before doing any tinting.

Figures 7.26 and 7.27 show examples of tinted photos. In Figure 7.26, the photo shown in Figure 7.24 now has the dull, yellowish tint of an old-fashioned sepia print. In Figure 7.27, the same photo has a pale, greenish-blue tint.

Figure 7.26 The photo in Figure 7.24 with sepia tinting.

Figure 7.27 The photo in Figure 7.24 with greenish-blue tinting.

Any command that adjusts hue and saturation can be used to tint a black and white photo. Paint Shop Pro's Black and White Points, when Preserve is unchecked, can also be used to tint a photo. Your image editor might also have one or more commands specifically designed to tint photos.

NOTE

> You can also tint a photo by adding a new layer above the photo, filling that layer with the color you want for your tinting, and then setting the blending mode of the upper layer to Color.

Colorizing Black and White

Have you seen photos from the 1950s where the photographer skillfully (or maybe not so skillfully) colorized a black and white photo by hand? You can get the same sort of effect by "painting" on top of your black and white digital photos (see Figure 7.28).

Figure 7.28 A black and white photo colored by hand (compare with original in Figure 7.5).

First, a new layer is added above the original black and white layer. The blending mode of the new layer is set to Color. Painting on the new layer then adds color without affecting the levels of lightness in the layer below. For the most control, each new color is added on its own layer (with the blending mode of each of these layers set to Color). That way, you can make adjustments to the color or opacity of an individual color layer without affecting any of the other layers.

Another way to combine color with black and white is to start out with a color photo, duplicate the original layer, desaturate the duplicate layer, and then erase any areas on the duplicate where you'd like the original color to show. This method can be used as an alternative to cropping (or in addition to cropping) to focus attention on a subject that might otherwise be lost in a busy composition (see Figure 7.29).

Figure 7.29 Two-layered photo where the top layer is desaturated, but the area over the main subject is erased.

Floating Color on Black and White

A nice effect can be created by "floating" a color photo on top of a larger black and white version, in effect allowing the photo to frame itself (see Figure 7.30).

To create this effect, start with a color photo. Duplicate the original layer, and then return to the original layer and desaturate it. On the duplicated layer, use your applications Transform or Deform tool to resize the layer so that the desaturated layer shows through along the edges. When you have the color layer at the size and position you want, add a drop shadow to make the smaller, color version appear to float above the black and white frame.

TIP

You can also get a good effect by using this method in reverse: Keep the lower layer in color and desaturate the upper layer. You might also try only partially desaturating the upper layer, allowing some of the original color to tint the upper layer.

Figure 7.30 A photo framed with a black and white version of itself.

Beyond Photo Correction

In the beginning of this chapter, we looked at some advanced photo correction techniques. In the last section, we started looking beyond mere photo correction and started experimenting with artistic photo manipulation. In Chapter 10, "Further Fun with Photos," we'll explore even more ways to do some creative editing with photos, including combining multiple photos into panoramas, montages, and other composites.

Mustangs

The white mare had fallen behind the herd. The stallion, seeing that he was short one mare, turned around to find her. She noticed almost immediately and ran to catch up. As she passed by him, he decided to make his point more aggressively and bit her on the flank. As is evident in this series of photos, she did not like this at all.

Donation Fund Established for Wild Horses and Burros

In response to the public's offers of donations to benefit wild horses and burros, the Bureau of Land Management (BLM)

Contributions will be used to purchase vaccines, antibiotics, milk for orphaned foals, and other items that will directly improve the health of wild

8

Sharing Your Work

Scrappers scrap to preserve memories and share them with others. This is true of digital scrappers no less than paper scrappers. For digital scrappers, the options available for sharing work include printing, posting to the Web, and saving to digital media such as CDs and DVDs. In this chapter, we'll explore each of these options.

On Paper

One way to share your digital layouts is to print them out and assemble them in physical scrapbooks. You can print the layouts yourself or have them done by a commercial printer. In this section, we'll outline what you need to know to get the best results for your printed layouts.

Image Size and Resolution for Printing

Whether you print your layouts yourself or have them printed commercially, you'll need to understand a little about image size and resolution. There's plenty of debate about what image resolution is best for printed layouts. One thing is certain—you need a lot of pixels to get a good print. Table 8.1 shows minimum pixel dimension recommendations provided at some online photo printing services.

Table 8.1 Recommended minimum pixel dimensions for prints

Pixel Dimensions	Maximum Print Size
1024 × 768	4 × 6 inches
1152 × 864	5 × 7 inches
1600 × 1200	8 × 10 inches (or larger)

You can calculate the pixel dimensions for your layout by multiplying the number of inches desired by the image resolution in pixels per inch (ppi). How many ppi should your image have? Here's where the controversy begins.

In numerous sources you'll find that 300 ppi is recommended for photo-quality print work, and some folks can be quite passionate about this setting. However, this old rule of thumb is coming into question. In fact, well-respected sources such as the National Association of Photoshop Professionals recommend 150 ppi for inkjet printing.

The difference between the number of pixels needed for an image with a resolution of 150 ppi and one with a resolution of 300 ppi is far from insignificant. Table 8.2 shows the pixel dimensions needed for images at 150 ppi, 200 ppi, and 300 ppi to be printed at some standard layout sizes.

Table 8.2 Pixel dimensions for prints at different image resolutions

Print Dimensions	150 ppi	200 ppi	300 ppi
8 × 8 inches	1200 × 1200	1600 × 1600	2400 × 2400
8 × 10 inches	1200 × 1500	1600 × 2000	2400 × 3000
8.5 × 11 inches	1275 × 1650	1700 × 2200	2550 × 3300
12 × 12 inches	1800 × 1800	2400 × 2400	3600 × 3600

For a 12 × 12 inch layout, the total number of pixels (in millions) needed are:

    150 ppi: 3.24

    200 ppi: 5.76

    300 ppi: 12.96

As you can see, the differences are considerable. A 12 × 12 inch layout created at 200 ppi has nearly twice as many pixels as one created at 150 ppi. One created at 300 ppi has more than twice as many pixels as one created at 200 ppi and about four times as many as one created at 150 ppi. That's a lot of pixels! So, if you don't need to use all the resources that a 300 ppi layout demands, there's no reason to go with 300 ppi.

Scrappers who submit their layouts to scrapbook magazines might respond, "But the magazines require 300 ppi." As you'll see later in this chapter, that doesn't mean you have to create your layouts at 300 ppi, even the ones you intend to submit to magazines. The magazines usually require submitted images to be smaller than full-size layouts. If you create your layout for full-size printing and then resize a copy of the image to submit for publication, you can modify the image resolution as well as the image dimensions at the same time, as many published scrappers do. Our recommendation is always to create your layouts at 200 ppi (or even 150 ppi if that resolution works to get you the results you want).

File Formats for Printing

The standard file format for commercially-printed photographic work is Tagged Image File Format (TIFF). Unless you're using a commercial printer who requires a different file format, TIFF is the format of choice for commercial print work. TIFF images can be compressed or uncompressed, but commercial printers usually require uncompressed files. If you compress your TIFF images to save disk space but your printer needs an uncompressed file, you can safely re-save the image in uncompressed mode because TIFF compression doesn't involve any loss of image data.

Online photo printers usually require JPEG files, although you need to be careful when you save a file in JPEG format. JPEG files involve a type of compression that throws image data away. Once that data is gone, there's no getting it back; each time you save a JPEG to disk and close the file, you lose more of your data. When you save a layout in JPEG format, you should save a copy, not the original. For archiving purposes, keep your original layout in your image editor's native format or in a format that uses lossless compression, such as TIFF or PNG. If you want to maintain the layer structure of your original layout, stick with your image editor's native format.

If you plan to print layouts yourself, you can use any of the file formats mentioned here.

Choosing the Right Desktop Printer

Any good photo-quality inkjet printer can be used to print your layouts. Perhaps the most popular models among scrappers are those from Canon, Epson, and HP. Any photo-quality printer can print layouts up to 8.5 × 11 inches. However, if you want to print your 12 × 12 inch layouts at home, you'll need a wide-format printer.

Good photo-quality printers can be purchased for about US$100 to $300. Wide-format printers can be considerably more expensive. Table 8.3 lists a few of the wide-format printers available.

Table 8.3 Wide-format photo-quality inkjet printers

Manufacturer	Model	Price (US)
Canon	i9100	$300
Canon	i9900	$500
Epson	Stylus Photo 1200	$400
Epson	Stylus Photo 2200	$700
HP	DeskJet 9650	$400
HP	DeskJet 9670	$500

Photo-quality printers use one of two types of ink: dye-based and pigment-based. Dye-based inks generally have the widest color ranges. Pigment-based inks generally produce the most water-resistant and fade-resistant prints, with Epson's UltraChrome inks purported to produce prints that last without fading for over 100 years when used with Epson's Premier Art Matte Scrapbook Photo Paper. When choosing your printer, be sure to check to see what type of ink it uses. Select a model that uses the sort of ink that has the characteristics that are most important to you.

NOTE

> Some printers have the option of using "photo gray" or "light black" ink in addition to or instead of standard black ink. This option might be important to you if you do a lot of black and white photo printing.

Sally uses an HP 9650 wide-format printer. Some of the things she likes about it are the price, the ease with which the paper tray can be adjusted, the "photo gray" ink option, and the special photo color ink cartridge with photo black ink. A couple things she doesn't like about it are that the color ink doesn't come in separate cartridges for each color and the fact that this large printer takes up a lot of desk space.

Lori is considering a Stylus Photo 2200. When she asked Ron Lacey, a long-time amateur photographer and contributor to www.psppower.com, what he thought of his Stylus Photo 2200, he gave it a big thumbs up, saying that it made stunning prints. He also said that he was impressed with prints from the Canon i9600. In addition, one nice feature both of these printers have is that they have separate ink cartridges for each color of ink.

What printer is right for you? When you go shopping for a printer, here are some things to keep in mind:

- Do you design your layouts larger than 8.5 × 11 inches? If so, you need a wide-format printer. If not, you'll probably want to stick with a standard photo-quality model, which will almost certainly cost less than a comparable wide-format model.

- Is maximum water-resistance and fade-resistance important to you? If so, choose a printer that uses pigment-based inks. Pigment-based inks can produce prints that, when printed on the proper paper and stored under proper conditions, should show no noticeable fading for 100 years or more.

- Do you do a lot of black and white photo printing? If so, consider a printer that uses photo gray or light black ink.

- Other things to consider are the physical size of the printer, the speed at which it prints, the noise level, and the cost of the type of ink and paper that the printer uses.

Choosing the Right Paper

The results you get when you print are highly dependent on the type of paper you use. A soft, porous paper produces blurry results. Colored paper affects the colors of your print. Paper that isn't bright white reduces the vividness of the print's colors. For these reasons, you'll normally want a paper that is coated and bright white.

If you want your printed layouts to have a long life, you'll also want your paper to be acid-free, lignin-free, and buffered. High-quality photo papers or specialty scrapbook papers (such as the ones available from Epson) will do the trick.

NOTE

> Specific papers are designed for specific inks, so you'll usually get the best results if you choose papers that are recommended for use with your printer's ink. Check your printer manufacturer's documentation or Web site for paper recommendations.

For layouts that are 8.5 × 11 inches or less, 8.5 × 11 inch paper is fine. For 12 × 12 inch layouts, you'll need either paper designed specifically for scrapbook layouts of this size or Super B media, which is 13 × 19 inches. If your paper is larger than your layouts, you can use a paper cutter to crop your print to the proper size.

TIP

When you use paper that's larger than your layout, there's no need to let that extra paper go to waste. Most image editors, photo album programs, and operating systems have a way to print multiple images on a single sheet of paper. Other images that you can use to fill the extra space include smaller versions of your layouts, journaling or elements that you can use on paper layouts, notes on what fonts and other resources you used to create your layout, or snapshots.

Resizing a Layout for Printing

If you've created your layout at the image resolution and pixel dimensions that you need for your printed version, then there's no need to resize. You don't even need to resize if you want to print smaller versions of your layout. Instead, you can tell your printer to scale the printed version to the proper size. For example, take a look at Figure 8.1, which shows the Print dialog box in PhotoPlus 9. In this example, the printer will print a layout created to be 12×12 inch (200 ppi) at 6×6 inches because Scale is set to 50%. The advantage to scaling, as opposed to resizing, is that with scaling your image is not changed in the slightest. All scaling does is tell the printer to print the image at a different size. (Note that the Print command in some image editors doesn't provide scaling as an option. Digital Image Pro 9, Paint Shop Pro 8.1, and PhotoPlus 9 are among the ones that do support scaling.)

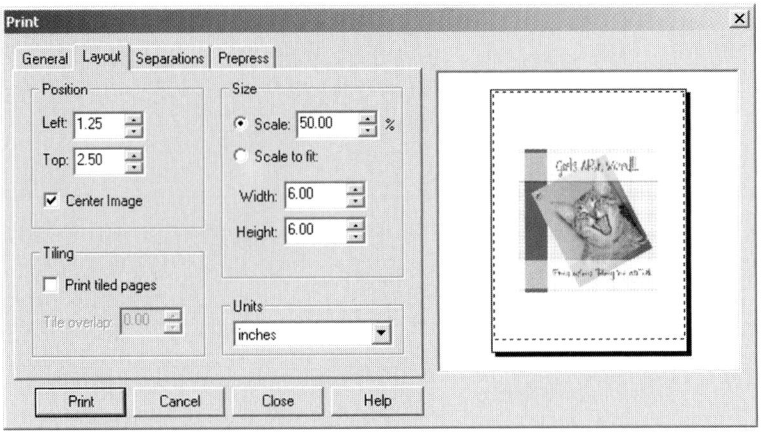

Figure 8.1 Scaling an image to 50% of its normal print size.

NOTE

As mentioned in Chapter 3, "Basic Layout Guidelines," when you anticipate situations in which you'll want your layout in multiple sizes, it's always better to start out with the largest size that you want and then reduce the image size for your copies. This holds true for scaling as well as resizing: scaling down usually produces better results than scaling up.

There are times when you really do want to change the actual size of an image. In these cases, you'll want to use your image editor's resizing command to resample the image.

Resampling changes an image. When you increase the size of an image, your image editor adds pixels in between existing pixels, making its best guess about what color those added pixels should be. When you decrease the size of an image, your image editor removes or combines pixels.

CAUTION

Once you resize an image and save it, you won't be able to get it back to the way it was before resizing. For this reason, it's best to keep an archive copy of your original image and to use another copy for your resized version.

Let's look at an example using PhotoImpact XL's Format > Image Size. PhotoImpact's Image Size dialog box is shown in Figure 8.2.

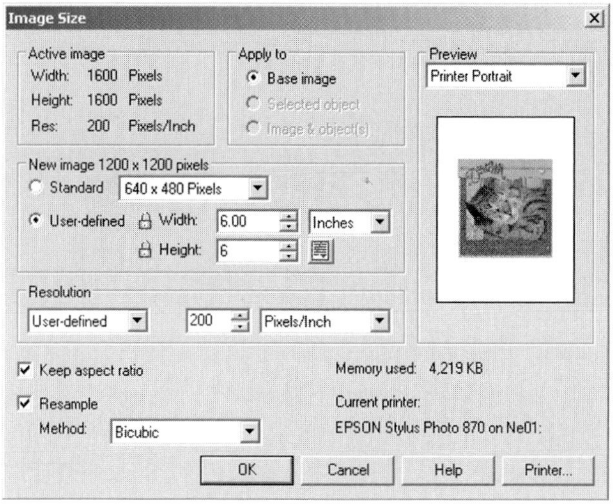

Figure 8.2 Resizing an image.

Here a layout that was originally 8 × 8 inches at 200 ppi is about to be resized to 6 × 6 inches at 200 ppi.

In whatever image editor you use, you should do the following when resizing an image:

- Select whatever setting ensures the aspect ratio of your image is maintained. If the aspect ratio is not maintained, the resulting image will be distorted.
- For images that you intend to print, be sure the resolution is set correctly. It's important that you select the resolution before trying to set the print size.
- After ensuring that the resolution is set correctly, set the print size that you want (in inches or centimeters).
- Choose a sampling method. A good general purpose resampling method for photo-like images is bicubic, but you should use whatever method the documentation for your image editor recommends for photographic images.

TIP

What should you do if you've created a layout at 200 ppi and want to submit it to a magazine that requires submissions at 300 ppi?

If your layout already has the required pixel dimensions for submission, you can simply invoke your image editor's resizing command and change the image resolution to 300 ppi without resampling. Doing so changes the image resolution without otherwise altering your image.

If your layout needs resizing as well as a change in image resolution, invoke the resizing command, set the resolution to 300 ppi, and then set either the print dimensions or the pixel dimensions to the required sizing for your submission. In this case, be sure to keep an archive copy of your original layout.

Printing an Image

Perhaps the easiest way to print your layout is to let your operating system handle things. For example, in Windows XP you can go to a folder in Windows Explorer that contains the image(s) you want to print, right-click on any image, and choose Print. You're presented with a wizard that walks you through the printing process. After the initial screen, you see the window shown in Figure 8.3, where you choose the image(s) you wish to print.

Click Next to go to a window where you can select printer options for your specific printer, and then choose the size at which to print each image and how many copies of each image to print. Figure 8.4 shows a selection for one copy of each of four selected images, all to be printed together on a single page, with each image printed at 3.5 × 5 inches.

Figure 8.3 Selecting photos to print in Windows XP Photo Printing Wizard.

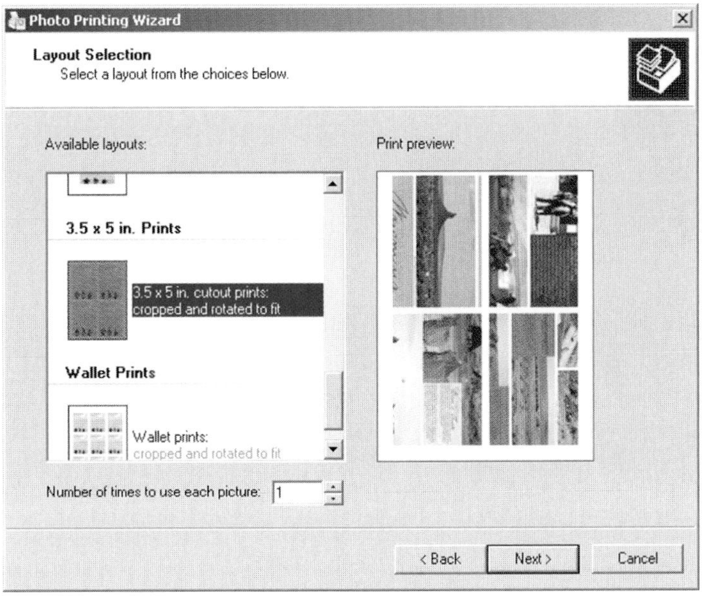

Figure 8.4 Determining print size and number of images per page in Windows XP Photo Printing Wizard.

Rather than printing directly from your operating system's print utility, you can print from within your image editor, photo album application, or page layout application.

Figure 8.5 shows Paint Shop Pro's Print dialog box. Here a 6 × 6 inch layout with an image resolution of 200 ppi is about to be printed without scaling. The Print dialog box for other image editors will be similar, but not identical. One thing they all have in common is the option of accessing your printer's properties. Figure 8.6 shows the Properties dialog box for the Epson 870 Stylus Photo printer.

In your image editor's Print dialog box, you set the size at which you want your image to be printed. In your printer's Properties dialog box, you indicate what type and size of paper to which you're printing (the "media") and what sort of print you're making (for example, a draft document, a high-quality photo, and so on). It's very important that you choose the proper settings for the printer properties in order to ensure that your print is made using the correct printer resolution.

In addition to printing single images on a page, most image editors also provide a facility for printing multiple images on a single page. For example, Paint Shop Pro has File > Print Layout, PhotoImpact has File > More Print Function > Print Multiple, PhotoPlus has File > Print Multiple, and Photoshop Elements has File > Print Layouts > Picture Package.

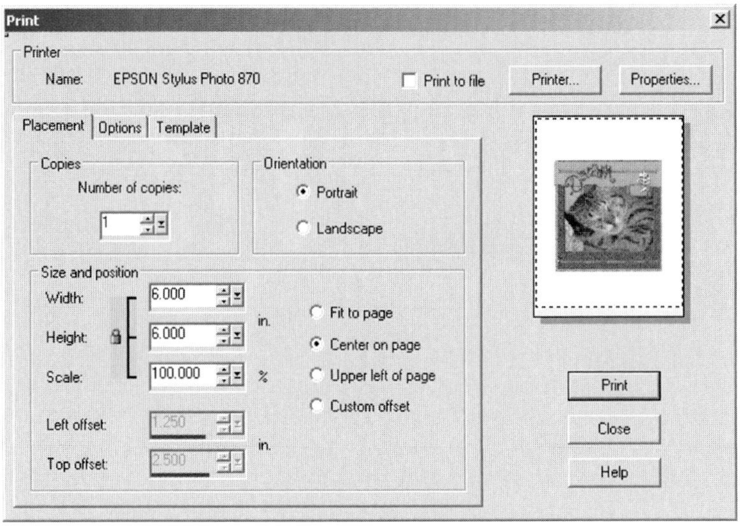

Figure 8.5 Print dialog box in Paint Shop Pro 8.1.

Figure 8.6 Properties dialog box for the Epson 870 Stylus Photo printer.

On the Web

Images destined for display on the Web are different from images for printing. First, Web images are much smaller than print images. Although your print layouts should normally be over 1,000 pixels high and wide, Web images should be no more than about 600 pixels in their largest dimension. Another difference is that only a few file formats can be displayed on a Web page. In addition, Web images are almost always compressed, while print images are usually not compressed.

GIF, JPEG, and PNG

Three file formats are generally supported for display in Web browsers: *Graphics Interchange Format* (GIF), *Joint Photographic Experts Group* (JPEG), and *Portable Network Graphics* (PNG):

■ GIF images have a limited palette of colors, from a minimum of 2 to a maximum of 256. The compression method used for GIF is lossless, which means that GIF compression doesn't involve loss of data. GIF compression favors solid blocks of colors (especially horizontal blocks) and therefore is best for images with sharp edges and few colors, such as line art and other simple drawings.

■ JPEG images can have up to 16.7 million colors. JPEG compression is lossy—when you compress a JPEG, you lose data. JPEG compression is best for images with many colors and subtle color shifts, such as photos and photorealistic images.

■ PNG has both a 256 paletted format and a 16.7 million color format. For images with solid blocks of color, the paletted format is best and may produce files that are smaller than comparable GIFs. For images with lots of colors and gradations, the 16.7 million color format is best. The PNG compression method is lossless—no data is lost with PNG compression—but PNGs are generally quite a bit larger than comparable JPEGs. Universal support for all PNG features is still not entirely established, and some Web browsers might have limited support for PNG. In fact, old Web browsers don't support PNG at all.

NOTE

Some folks make the mistake of thinking that JPEG is always the best format for any Web graphic. However, JPEG versions of images that are best suited for GIF compression usually have larger file sizes and generally show degraded image quality when compared to their GIF counterparts.

Photos and scrapbook layouts generally are best saved as JPEGS, but as you'll see later in this chapter, GIF is sometimes useful for scrappers as well.

Resizing a Layout for the Web

File size is an important consideration for your Web images because file size largely determines the amount of time it takes to download and display your Web images. For that reason, you want the pixel dimensions of your Web images to be much smaller than the dimensions of the print versions of your layouts. A good rule of thumb is to keep the largest dimension of layouts intended for the Web at 600 pixels or less.

When resizing images for the Web, resolution really isn't important, only pixel dimensions matter. For Web images, don't worry about resizing settings that affect print size, just set the size in terms of pixel dimensions.

Optimizing Images for the Web

Pixel dimensions alone don't determine file size. File format and compression play their part too. For photos and photorealistic images like the layout shown in Figure 8.7, the JPEG file format will give you the best image quality at the smallest file size.

When you save a JPEG version of your layout, you have control over how much compression to use. Different image editors express the amount of JPEG compression in different ways. Digital Image Pro has a quality scale from 1 to 100, with 1 yielding lowest quality and smallest file size and 100 yielding highest quality and largest file size. Paint Shop Pro 8.1 has a compression level scale of 1 to 99, with 1 yielding highest quality and largest file size and 99 yielding lowest quality and smallest file size. PhotoImpact XL and Photoshop Elements 2.0 have a quality scale from 0 to 100, with 0 yielding lowest quality and smallest file size and 100 yielding highest quality and largest file size.

When you optimize a JPEG, nearly all image editors provide you with a preview of the result, its file size, and an estimate of download time. Try for a file size of no more than

Figure 8.7 A layout best suited for the JPEG file format.

about 150K, with a download time no more than 20 to 25 seconds. Twenty-five seconds might not sound like much, but it seems like a long time to a visitor to your Web site who's waiting for your image to download.

There's always a trade-off between file size and image quality. When you're optimizing your layouts, try for the smallest file size that doesn't sacrifice too much quality.

TIP

> If your image editor lets you save your JPEGs in either Standard format or Progressive format, you might want to give Progressive a try. Progressive JPEGs almost always have smaller file sizes than comparable Standard versions.

Most layouts are not suitable to save in GIF format. Although GIF compression is lossless, GIF supports only a maximum of 256 colors, which is often not enough for photos or photorealistic images. Even when photo-like images look fine as GIFs, the file size is usually much larger for photos saved as GIFs compared to JPEG. However, in the next section, you'll see one case in which it can pay to save at least part of your layout in GIF format.

Image Slicing

Large images can be sliced into several smaller images and then reassembled using an HTML table, making the collection of smaller images look like a single large image. You may have heard that slicing a large image reduces download time, but generally this is not really the case. In fact, sliced images can take longer to download than a single large image. One advantage of sliced images is that there is often a psychological effect. Even if the download time is not reduced, people viewing your Web page may feel as though the download time is faster because they have parts of the image to look at while the other parts are still loading.

Another advantage of image slicing is that it allows you to save some sections of your image in GIF format and other sections in JPEG format. This can be particularly useful for layouts that have large blocks of solid colors and text in some areas of the page and photographs in other areas. Figure 8.8 shows a perfect example being sliced with Paint Shop Pro 8.1's Image Slicer.

In this case, the image can be sliced into three pieces: the large block of color at the top, the photograph in the middle, and the text area on the bottom. The top and bottom slices will have the best quality and the smallest file sizes when saved in GIF format, while the middle slice optimizes best in JPEG format.

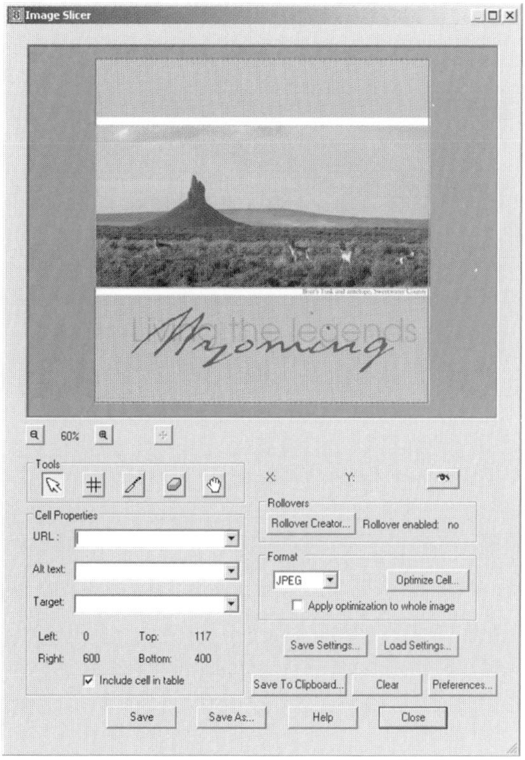

Figure 8.8 Slicing a large image into several smaller images using Paint Shop Pro's Image Slicer.

You don't need to know HTML to create a sliced image. Image slicers not only slice the image into pieces, but create the HTML code for you. Then, you can just copy the generated code and paste it into your own Web page. Figure 8.9 shows the result for the sample image.

Web Photo Galleries

Some photo editors and nearly all photo album applications include a way of generating Web galleries like the one shown in Figure 8.10. A gallery is made up of a collection of thumbnails linked to full-size images that are displayed one at a time. Click a thumbnail, and the corresponding full-size image is displayed.

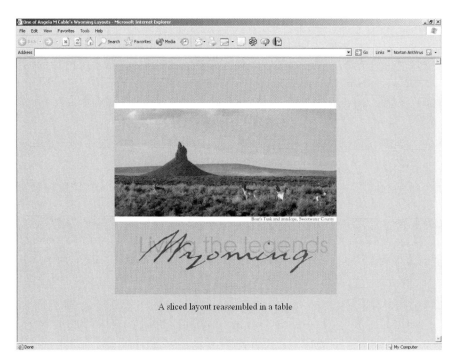

Figure 8.9 A sliced image displayed on a Web page.

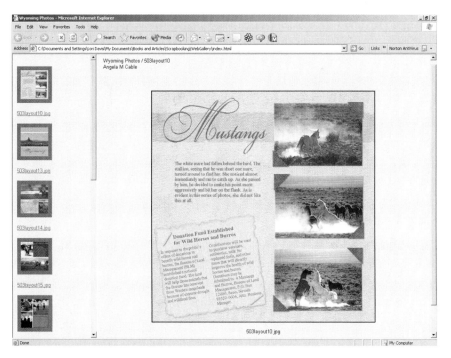

Figure 8.10 A Web gallery.

This example was generated using File > Create Web Photo Gallery in Photoshop Elements 2.0, and simple galleries can also be created with PhotoImpact XL's File > Export > Web Album. You can create Web galleries with photo album applications such as Adobe's Photoshop Album, Jasc's Paint Shop Photo Album, and Ulead's Photo Explorer. As with image slicers, Web gallery generators produce all the HTML code you need. You simply provide information that the generator requests, and it does the work of producing the thumbnails and Web pages.

Web Slideshows

A slideshow is a collection of images displayed one after another, somewhat like a slideshow presented with an old-fashioned slide projector. A Web slideshow is similar, except that your images are displayed in a Web browser, and the progression from one image to another is either made automatically or controlled by the person viewing the slideshow. Figure 8.11 shows an example, created in PhotoImpact XL with File > Export > Web Slide Show.

Once again, as with image slicers and Web gallery generators, you don't need to know any HTML to create a Web slideshow. The slideshow generator itself creates all the HTML code you need.

Figure 8.11 A Web slideshow generated in PhotoImpact XL.

Displaying Your Layouts on the Web

To share your layouts on the Web, you'll need some Web space.

One possibility is to have your own Web site. This is the option you'll need if you want to display sliced images, Web galleries, and slideshows that you create yourself. Check to see if your Internet Service Provider (ISP) gives you free space for a Web site. If not, there are plenty of low-cost alternatives, such as Web communities like Angelfire (www.angelfire.com) and Tripod (www.tripod.com). Some places provide free space if you agree to allow them to display banner ads on your site. Even if you want to avoid ads, the cost can be quite reasonable, often in the range of US$5 per month.

If you don't have a Web page of your own and don't want one, you still have some options:

■ You can display individual layouts in albums on photo sites such as Ofoto (www.ofoto.com), Snapfish (www.snapfish.com), and Shutterfly (www.shutterfly.com). For this option, you'll need to register at the site, but registration is free. Then, you can upload your layouts in JPEG format to your own albums, where your friends can view your creations.

■ You can display individual layouts in your own personal gallery at an online scrapbook site, such as Digital Scrapbook Place (www.digitalscrapbookplace.com), Pages of the Heart (www.pagesoftheheart.net), and Scrapbook Bytes (www.scrapbook-bytes.com). You'll need to register at the site, but you'll probably want to anyway, to gain full access to the site's other benefits.

Sending Layouts as E-mail Attachments

Another way to share your layouts with family and friends is to send your layouts as e-mail attachments. Most image editors, photo album applications, and the collage-generating FotoFusion from LumaPix, all include commands for sending images as e-mail attachments. Figure 8.12 shows a layout about to be sent as e-mail from within FotoFusion.

Be very careful about the file size of the images you send via e-mail, especially if the recipient doesn't have a high-speed Internet connection. Unless you know that the recipient can deal with larger files, stick to the same rules of thumb as for Web images: keep the maximum pixel dimension to about 600 pixels and keep the file size at about 150K or less.

TIP

As a courtesy to others, don't send e-mail attachments to folks who aren't expecting them. When in doubt, it's always best to ask first before sending files as e-mail attachments.

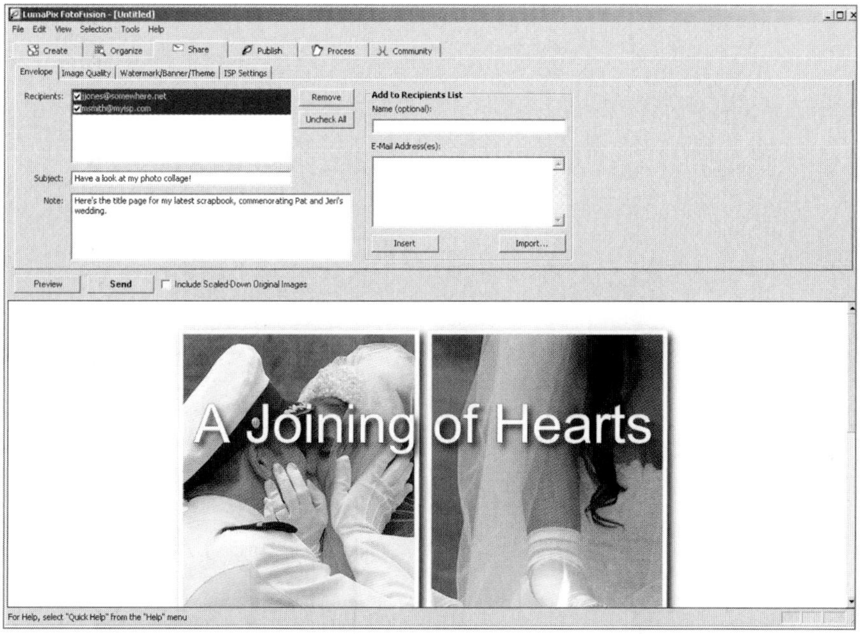

Figure 8.12 Sending a layout via e-mail from within FotoFusion.

On Digital Media

In addition to printing your digital layouts or posting them on a Web site, you can burn your layouts to CD or DVD. This can be as simple as putting copies of your collection of layouts on digital media for archiving purposes. Or, you can copy your Web photo galleries and slideshows to digital media to share with your family and friends, who can then view your work on their computers using their HTML browser. Another possibility is to create slideshows that are specifically designed for digital media and that can be viewed either on a computer or a TV using a DVD player that can play video CDs or writable DVDs.

Photo album applications and some image editors include ways to create documents on digital media. For example, PhotoImpact's Web Album and Web Slide Show include options for burning to digital media. In this way, you can create an entire digital scrapbook, burn it to CD or DVD, and distribute copies to all your family and friends.

NOTE

Digital media slideshows can be quite sophisticated. This is especially true of those generated by photo album applications, where you can add captions, fancy transitions, a music soundtrack, or any combination of these features.

9

Creating Your Own Elements

In this chapter, we'll explore how you can create your own scrapbook elements, including papers, mats, frames, tags, brads, eyelets, and fibers. In general, you'll want to create your elements at the largest size you're likely to need them (for example, maybe half an inch for a brad or eyelet, or three inches in diameter for a circular tag). Create your elements at 200 ppi or whatever image resolution you normally use for your layouts. Elements that include transparency should be saved in your image editor's native file format or in another format that supports transparency, such as PNG. Background papers should be saved as JPEG, TIF, or PNG.

Using Clip Art

Clip art is ready-made art that you can incorporate into your own designs. Some clip art comes in the form of vector-based line drawings like the Microsoft Office clip art shown in Figure 9.1. Some are scans of physical line drawings, such as the Dover Art example shown in Figure 9.2, while others are figures isolated from photos, such as the Hemera Photo Objects example shown in Figure 9.3 (where the checkerboard pattern isn't part of the image, but simply indicates transparency).

If your image editor supports vector editing, vector-based clip art can be resized, recolorized, and otherwise manipulated without any distortion at all. However, even if your image editor doesn't have full support for vectors, you may be able to open vector images and use them in raster format. In that case, you lose the advantages of vectors, but you still can make use of the images.

Figure 9.1 Vector-based clip art from Microsoft Office.

Figure 9.2 Scanned clip art from Dover Art.

Figure 9.3 Photo object from Hemera.

Scanned clip art is raster-based and is usually made available in one or more of these image formats: BMP, GIF, JPEG, or TIF. Often this sort of clip art could use a little clean-up, as the close-up indicates in Figure 9.4.

To get rid of jaggy edges in scanned black and white clip art, touch up any straight edges with a hard-edged square brush. For curves, try this method:

Figure 9.4 Scanned clip art sometimes needs some cleaning up.

1. If necessary, use your image editor's straightening or Deform/Transform tool to straighten the image.

2. Touch up any obvious gaps or dust spots with your paintbrush.

3. Blur the image slightly with Gaussian Blur.

4. Increase the contrast to get smooth edges using Levels, as shown in Figure 9.5. Moving the left slider to the right maximizes the dark areas, while moving the right slider to the left maximizes white areas.

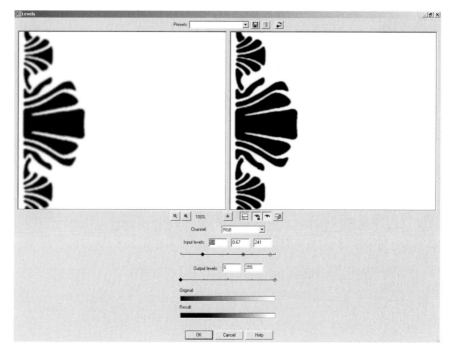

Figure 9.5 Using Levels to create smooth edges.

Notice the difference between what you see in Figure 9.4 and the cleaned-up version shown in Figure 9.6. The image is improved greatly—and with very little effort.

So what can you do with clip art? You can use colored drawings, line art that you color by hand, and photo objects like stickers, pasting them on your page as accents. However, there's more to clip art than stickers. You can also use clip art as the basis for brads, frames, and other elements, or to decorate papers and tags.

Figure 9.6 Cleaned-up version.

Backgrounds and Papers

The foundation of any layout is the background. In this section, we'll look at how to simulate cardstock, patterned paper, and corrugated backgrounds. You'll also see how to create vellum and torn paper.

Simulating Cardstock

Probably the easiest way to create simulated cardstock for a background is to open an image the size of your finished layout. Fill the entire canvas area with the color you want, and then apply a texture to the fill. Different effects can be achieved with different textures or by combining textures. You can also create textures by adding some noise to your colored paper, and then applying effects and adjustments such as embossing and blurring. Experiment to see what effects you can create.

NOTE

The term *texture* is used in many image editors to refer to simulated surface textures, and that's the meaning here. However, some image editors, such as PhotoImpact, follow the lead of 3D imaging programs and use texture to refer to what most image editors call a *pattern*. In a case like that, what we refer to here as texture is called a *bump* or *bump map*.

If your image editor supports layer blending modes, you can also add objects that seem to be embedded in your paper. First, create a layer of textured paper. Then add a new layer and place some of the objects that you want to appear embedded in your paper. Add texture to the new layer, then change the blending mode of this layer to Overlay or Soft Light, and adjust the layer opacity until you get the effect you want. If you like, add more layers, each with its own set of objects and blending mode and opacity settings. If the objects on a particular layer appear too distinct, add a blur to that layer. When you're done, you can merge all the layers into a single layer. Figure 9.7 shows an example of a textured paper with embedded objects.

Figure 9.7 Simulated textured paper with embedded objects.

Simple Patterned Paper with Seamless Tiling

Creating a background that's the same size as your finished layout might often be easy, but it certainly isn't efficient. Images with resolutions of say 200 ppi that are 8.5 × 11 inch or 12 × 12 inch take up an awful lot of disk space. For the sake of your hard drive if for nothing else, a far better approach is to create seamless tiles.

A *seamless tile* is a small pattern that you can use to fill a large space. It has no noticeable seam, so the tile can be repeated up and down and across the space without any hint that the whole patterned area is made up of many copies of a single tile. Suppose you want to make a tile from an image like the one in Figure 9.8. If you were to use this image as a tile, the result would be what you see in Figure 9.9, where the edges of the individual tiles are quite distinct.

Figure 9.8 An image from which to create a tiling pattern.

Figure 9.9 Original image used as a tile.

If the tile were seamless, you'd get something like what you see in Figure 9.10, a much more pleasing effect.

There are several ways to make a seamless tile. Many image editors include some means of creating a seamless tile from an image. For example, Paint Shop Pro users have Effects > Image Effects > Seamless Tiling, PhotoImpact users have Web > Create Seamless Tile (which requires that you make a selection before applying the effect), and PhotoPlus users have Effects > Other > Tile Maker. These sorts of seamless tiling effects sometimes give less than satisfactory results. For some images, you'll get better results if you use a more hands-on method using an offset filter, which is how the tile shown in Figure 9.10 was made.

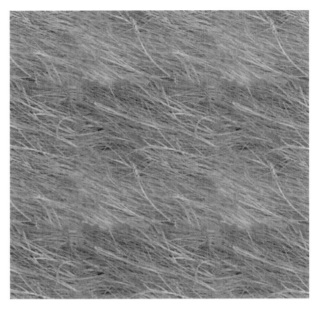

Figure 9.10 Seamless tile.

Most image editors include an offset filter. Here are some examples:

Paint Shop Pro 8.1

Effects > Image Effects > Offset

PhotoPlus 9

Effects > Distort > Offset

Photoshop Elements 2.0

Filter > Other > Offset

If your image editor doesn't include an offset filter, you can download Half Wrap, one of Sandy Blair's free Simple Filter plug-ins at www.btinternet.com/~cateran/simple/.

What you want to do with the offset filter is split your image into quarters and then swap the quarters so that each of the corners appears in the middle of the image. Half Wrap does this automatically. For more complex offset filters, you'll need to choose settings so that the horizontal offset is half the width of your image and the vertical offset is half the height of your image. You'll also need to choose a mode that causes the offset image to wrap around. (In Paint Shop Pro, set Edge Mode to Wrap; in PhotoPlus and Photoshop Elements, set Undefined Areas to Wrap Around.) Figure 9.11 shows

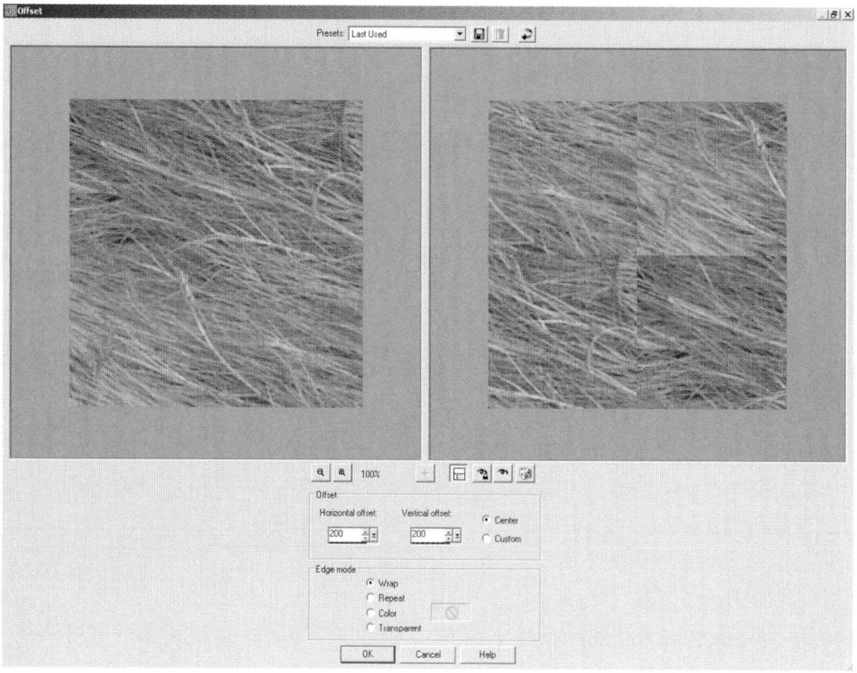

Figure 9.11 Using an offset filter.

what you'd see in Paint Shop Pro, using the example image from Figure 9.8.

After applying the offset filter, the real work begins. Now use your clone brush, smudge brush, or paintbrush to blend together the areas around the seams running up and down and across the offset image, as shown in Figure 9.12.

Keep in mind that patience pays off when doing this touch-up work, and that you might want to zoom in on your image. Change the size and opacity of the brush as needed, and when using the clone brush, reset the sampling area often. Be careful to avoid painting over the edge of

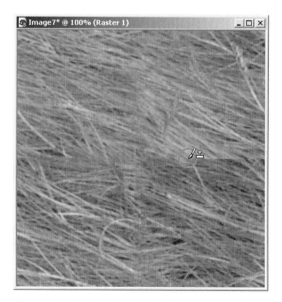

Figure 9.12 Getting rid of the seams with the clone brush.

the image canvas because doing so will create new seams. When you have the results you want, you might want to apply the offset filter again, partly to set the image back to its original orientation and partly to check that no new seams were introduced.

NOTE

> Several plug-in filters are available for producing abstract seamless tiles or tiles that simulate natural textures. Some of Sandy Blair's Simple Filters are examples of the first type, and many of Alien Skin's Eye Candy and Xenofex filters have a setting that produces seamless tiling effects.
>
> You can also get some nice natural texture tiles by scanning objects such as cloth and paper and then using the offset method to make a portion of the scanned image seamless.

TIP

> Seamless tiles should be saved as JPEGs if the pattern contains subtle color grada-tions, like the grass in the example tile. For tiles that are made up of solid blocks of color with distinct edges, like the stripes and plaids you'll make in the next section, you may get better results saving as a TIF, BMP, or paletted PNG.

The method for filling an image or selection with a seamless tile varies from image edi-tor to image editor. Here's a summary of how to use your seamless tiles in some of the popular image editors:

Digital Image Pro 9 has no native way of filling an area with a pattern. But Digital Image Pro users shouldn't despair because they can download Redfield's Seamless Workshop plug-in filter at www.redfieldplugins.com. (A copy is also available on the book's CD.) To use the tile, copy the tile image to your project and position it in the upper left corner of the image canvas. Apply the Seamless Workshop plug-in, adjusting the Tile Edge Location controls until the tiles line up with no spaces between them. Click the Make Filled Pattern button to apply the tiled pattern.

Paint Shop Pro 8.1 lets you use patterns or any open image as a tile. Choose the Flood Fill tool. Click the foreground swatch on the Materials palette, go to the Pat-tern tab, and select your tile. If the tile image is open or if you saved the tile in your Patterns folder, the tile appears in the pattern selection list. Once you've selected your tile, click in your image canvas with Flood Fill to fill with the pattern.

PhotoImpact XL allows you to apply any image file as a pattern with the Fill command. Choose Edit > Fill, and then select the tile by its file name.

PhotoPlus 9 lets you fill with any saved pattern. To save your tile as a pattern, open the tile image and choose Edit > Create Pattern, placing the tile in whatever pattern category you feel is appropriate. To use the tile, choose Edit > File, select Pattern as the Type, and click the pattern swatch to bring up the selection list. If you don't see the tile in the selection list, right-click one of the thumbnails, and then select the category in which you placed your tile. Select the tile and click OK.

Photoshop Elements 2.0 also has a Fill command. Choose Edit > Fill, select Pattern, and select the pattern you want. Only images that have been defined previously as patterns are available. To define an image as a pattern, open the image and choose Edit > Define Pattern.

Stripes and Plaids

It's easy to make seamless tiles for repeating stripes, and not much harder to make gingham or plaid tiles. For vertical stripes, open an image as wide as you'll need for

Figure 9.13 A simple two-colored stripe tile.

the repeating pattern of stripes. The image doesn't have to be very tall—in fact, one pixel would be sufficient, although you'll probably want it taller just so you can better see what you're doing. Add colored rectangles to your image for each of the stripes in the pattern. Figure 9.13 shows a simple two-colored example tile, and Figure 9.14 shows the result of using the tile to fill an area.

Figure 9.14 An area filled with the stripe tile.

For horizontal stripes, you do pretty much the same thing. The difference is that you make the image tall enough to accommodate the repeating pattern, making it just wide enough for you to see what you're doing.

For a gingham pattern, begin with a square image canvas large enough for the repeating pattern. Add a colored rectangle, as shown in Figure 9.15. Duplicate the layer and rotate only the duplicated layer 90°. Lower the transparency of the duplicated layer to 50%. The result will look something like what you see in Figure 9.16. When used as a pattern to fill an area, this tile yields the results in Figure 9.17.

You create plaids as you do gingham, but you use more stripes. Begin with a square image canvas large enough for the repeating pattern, and then add some stripes, as

Figure 9.15 The basis of the gingham pattern.

Figure 9.16 Result of duplicating the layer, rotating it, and reducing the opacity.

Figure 9.17 An area filled with the gingham pattern.

shown in Figure 9.18. As with gingham, duplicate the layer and rotate only the duplicated layer 90°. Lower the transparency of the duplicated layer to 50%. The result will look something like Figure 9.19. When used as a pattern to fill an area, this tile yields the results in Figure 9.20.

Save your striped, plaid, and gingham patterns as BMPs, TIFs, or paletted PNGs. This avoids getting murky areas called "artifacts" that could result if these sorts of images are saved as JPEGs. For PhotoPlus and Photoshop Elements, be sure to save your tiles as patterns. These tiles are seamless, so there's no need to do anything further to them.

Figure 9.18 Basis of the plaid pattern.

Figure 9.19 Result of duplicating the layer, rotating it, and reducing the opacity.

Figure 9.20 An area filled with the plaid pattern.

TIP

You can also add a texture to your stripe, gingham, and plaid backgrounds. For the most flexibility, don't save the texture to your tiles, but instead apply the texture to the filled area. This way, you can use different textures for different layouts without having to save multiple versions of your tiles.

Corrugated Cardboard

To create a corrugated cardboard tile, you simply need to create an image that's filled with a gradient like the one shown in Figure 9.21.

Notice how the gradient goes from dark to light, and then from light to dark. When this tile fills an area, it looks like a series of raised and indented bands, as shown in Figure 9.22.

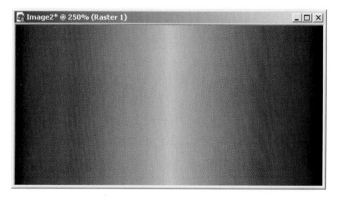

Figure 9.21 A gradient tile for simulating corrugated cardboard.

Figure 9.22 An area filled with the corrugated pattern.

To create a corrugation tile, you need an image only as wide as one repetition of the corrugation. Fill this image with an appropriate gradient, and then save the image for use as a pattern.

Here's how to fill the tile image with a gradient in some popular image editors:

- **Digital Image Pro 9.** After inserting a rectangle in your project, resize the rectangle to the size of the tile, set the Line Thickness to None, and choose Format > Shape or Line > Fill Color. Click Gradient. Choose the appropriate color pattern and style, and then click Done.

- **Paint Shop Pro 8.1.** Open an image the size of your tile. On the Materials palette, click the foreground swatch, go to the Gradient tab, and choose the appropriate gradient. Click in the image canvas with Flood Fill.

- **PhotoImpact XL.** Open an image the size of your tile. Choose the Linear Gradient Fill tool. On the Color Panel, choose the gradient you want, and then drag across the image canvas and release the mouse button.

- **PhotoPlus 9.** Open an image the size of your tile. Choose the Rectangular Selection tool and select the left side of the image. Fill the selection with the appropriate gradient using the Gradient Fill tool. Copy the selection and paste as a new layer. Turn off the selection, and then choose Image > Flip Horizontally > Layer. Line up the two layers. Crop, if needed, to eliminate any empty areas in the image canvas. Merge the layers.

- **Photoshop Elements 2.0.** Open an image the size of your tile. Choose the Gradient tool. On the tool options bar, choose Reflected Gradient. Click in the center of your image canvas and drag to the right edge. Release the mouse button.

TIP

A gradient of dark and light grays is fine for a corrugation tile. You can fill an area with the tile, and then colorize the corrugated area as needed for your particular layout.

Simulating Vellum

Vellum is extremely easy to make. Open a new image with a transparent background. Place a rectangle in your image canvas, using whatever color you want for your vellum. Lower the transparency of the layer, so that the rectangle is semi-transparent, as shown in Figure 9.23 (where the checkerboard pattern isn't part of the image, but only indicates transparency).

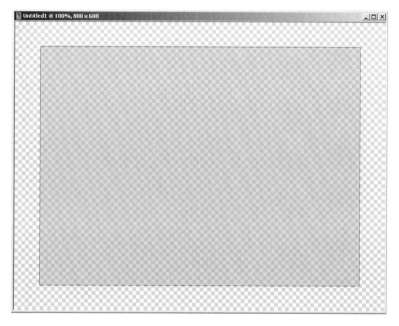

Figure 9.23 Create vellum by lowering the opacity of a colored area.

TIP

When you use the vellum in your layouts, you'll get distinct edges and a nice 3D effect if you add a slight drop shadow to the vellum.

You can also get a more realistic effect by adding a layer above the vellum, filling an area the size of the vellum with a black and white linear gradient set at about 45°, and setting the blending mode to Soft Light.

Torn Paper

It's easy to get a torn paper effect. Open the image that contains your paper, and then with your image editor's Freehand Selection tool ("lasso"), make a rough, jagged selection along the edge where you want the tear, as shown in Figure 9.24.

Figure 9.24 Begin with a jagged freehand selection.

Delete the selection and turn the selection off. Then make a new jagged selection that extends into the torn edge and almost, but not quite, matches the shape of the edge, as shown in Figure 9.25.

Reduce the saturation and increase the brightness of the selection, and then deselect. The result looks something like Figure 9.26, where a drop shadow was also added.

TIP

> The lightened and desaturated part of the torn edge can be made to look more worn by adding a little noise and blurring it a bit. Other variations you can try are running a Soften brush along the part of the paper where the solid paper meets the tear, using a Smudge brush to blend the area where the solid paper meets the tear, or running a warp tool along the tear to make it even more irregular.

Figure 9.25 Make a new jagged selection within the torn edge.

Figure 9.26 Simulated torn paper (with added drop shadow).

Mats and Frames

Creating mats and frames is much like creating a background. You begin just as you would for a background: Open the image at the size you want, and then either choose a color and apply a texture or fill the image with a seamless pattern. What you do next depends on whether you want to plop your photo on top of a simple mat or make the photo appear as though it's placed behind a cutout in a frame.

Simple Mats

Create a rectangular image the size that you want for your mat. Fill with the color you want and add a texture if you like. You might want to bevel the edges of the mat a bit, although this usually isn't necessary. In your layout, you can simply add a drop shadow to the mat to give it a 3D appearance. You should add your photo on a layer above the mat and add a slight drop shadow to the photo as well, to make it appear to lie on top of the mat.

Creating Cutouts for Frames

For a frame that lies on top of your photo, with the photo showing through a cutout in the frame, begin just as you do for a mat: Create a rectangular image the size of your frame, fill with the color you want, and add a texture if you want your frame to be textured. Then use your selection tool to define a rectangular or elliptical selection within the frame and delete the contents of the selection (see Figure 9.27).

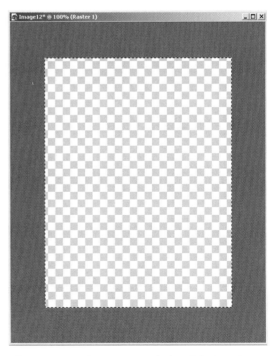

Figure 9.27 A cutout made by deleting the contents of a selection.

Figure 9.28 Example of a finished frame in use.

Place the frame on a layer above your photo. Add a bevel to the inside of the frame by darkening the upper left and lightening the lower right a bit. (Instructions for how to do this in different image editors are included on the CD.) Then add a drop shadow to the frame to make it look like it's lying above the background and the photo. The result is shown in Figure 9.28.

Fancier Mats and Frames

Not all mats and frames are rectangular. For oval mats and frames, use the same methods that you use for rectangular mats and frames, but start out with an oval rather than a rectangle. For really fancy mats and frames, start out with a piece of clip art or a character from a dingbat font set. To get 3D-looking frames, you can colorize and apply bevels to black and white clip art or dingbats, either alone or in combination with other shapes. A couple examples are shown in Figure 9.29.

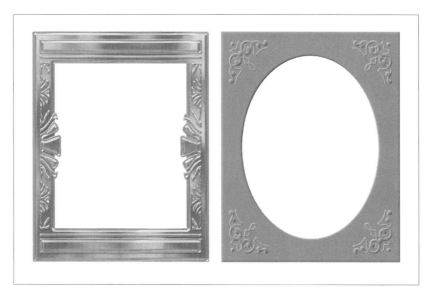

Figure 9.29 Frames made using clip art (left) and a dingbat (right). Clip art from Dover Publications' Art Nouveau Frames and Borders; dingbat from House of Lime DBL Corners.

Tags

Now let's take a look at how to create simple rectangle-based tags. (Tutorials for making round metal-rimmed tags are included on the CD.) You can make a simple packing tag like the one in Figure 9.30 by first drawing a rectangle for the main body of the tag, and then drawing a smaller rectangle for the top of the tag. Use your image editor's shape-editing tool or Deform/Transform tool to shrink the top of the rectangle so that the sides angle in. If these shapes are on separate layers, merge the layers once you have the shapes lined up correctly. Then you only need to cut out a hole near the top of the tag, and add any texturing or shadowing that you want.

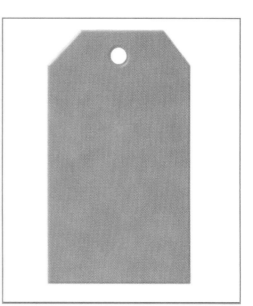

Figure 9.30 A simple packing tag.

You can make a rounded-top rectangular tag in much the same way: Draw a rectangle for the main body of the tag, and then draw a circle or ellipse for the top of the tag. Align these two shapes, merge the layers if the shapes are on separate layers, cut out a hole, and add a texture or shadowing if you like.

TIP

> You can add decorations to your tags using clip art or dingbat characters. For example, you can make simple clip art or dingbats look stamped onto your tag by adding the clip art or dingbat to its own layer, applying a texture to that layer, and using a blending mode such as Multiply or Overlay to blend the "stamp" onto the tag.

Brads and Eyelets

Brads and eyelets are some of the easiest elements to make, especially if your image editor has a facility for creating 3D-looking spheres or rings, such as Paint Shop Pro's Balls and Bubbles effect and Magnifying Lens effect or PhotoImpact's 3D modes for the Path Drawing and Outline Drawing tools.

If your image editor doesn't have built-in 3D effects, you can still create some nice-looking brads and eyelets. Next, a general method for each is described, with specific methods for creating brads and eyelets in several popular image editors included on the CD.

TIP

> In general when creating brads and eyelets, start out with an image canvas of about half an inch by half an inch, set at the image resolution you normally use for your layouts. Be sure the background of the new image is transparent, and save the image as a PNG with transparency.

For a brad, create a circle centered in the image canvas. Fill it with a sunburst gradient with a highlight in the upper left and with highlights and shadows added with the Dodge and Burn tools, or use whatever means your image editor provides for simulating a 3D sphere.

For an eyelet, create a ring shape and add beveling to the ring, either with the Dodge and Burn tools or with a beveling effect if your image editor has one. If you can't make a ring directly, make a circle and then cut out a smaller, circular selection within the larger circle. Figure 9.31 shows a few examples created with Paint Shop Pro, PhotoImpact, and Photoshop Elements.

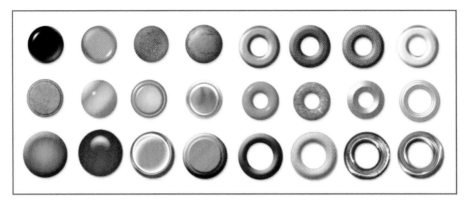

Figure 9.31 Sample brads and eyelets (top: Paint Shop Pro; middle: PhotoImpact; bottom: Photoshop Elements).

In addition to round brads and eyelets, you should try some other shapes as well. In any image editor, you can draw a shape and cut out a hole. Then, you can add beveling shadows and highlights by hand or with a bevel effect if your image editor has a facility for adding bevels. Another option for bevels is to use a plug-in filter such as Bevel Boss, Glass, or Chrome, which are all included in Alien Skin Software's Eye Candy (a demo of which is included on the CD). Figure 9.32 shows some examples of fancy brads and eyelets with bevels made using Alien Skin's Eye Candy filters.

Figure 9.32 A few fancy brads and eyelets.

TIP

The shapes used for fancy brads and eyelets can also be made using clip art shapes or dingbat font characters. Copy and paste a clip art shape to its own layer or enter a character from a dingbat font, and then apply a bevel. (For font characters, you may first need to render the text—that is, convert it to raster—in order to apply a bevel or other effects.)

Ribbons and Fibers

Ribbons and fibers add some of the nicest additions to a layout, and it takes little effort to create them. Ribbons are basically patterned rectangles, and fibers are simply fancy lines.

Ribbons

Figure 9.33 shows a segment of basic gingham ribbon. To make such a ribbon, open a new image with a transparent background that's slightly taller than you want your ribbon to be. Add a rectangle that extends from the left side of the rectangle to the right. Fill the rectangle with a gingham pattern. Then on a new layer, add a thin solid-colored rectangle across the top of the patterned rectangle and on another new layer add a thin solid-colored rectangle across the bottom of the patterned rectangle (see Figure 9.34).

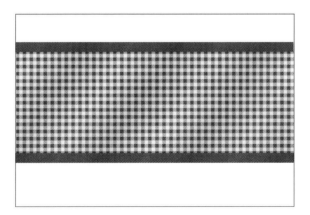

Figure 9.33 Basic gingham ribbon.

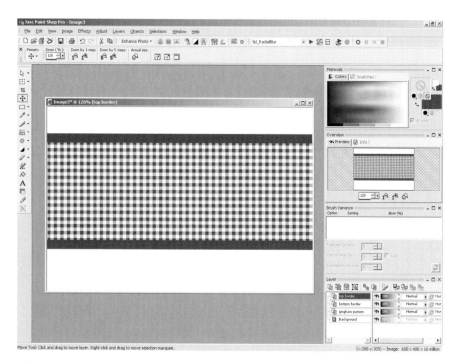

Figure 9.34 Add the ribbon's borders as long, thin rectangles on separate layers.

Add a slight bevel to each of the thin rectangles. For the top thin rectangle, add a subtle drop shadow going straight down. For the bottom thin rectangle, add a subtle drop shadow going straight up. Merge the layers, and then add some shading, either with your Burn brush, or with a texturing or lighting filter available in your image editor. You can also give the ribbon a more natural look by running a warp brush over it or applying a plug-in filter, such as Eye Candy's Jiggle or Xenofex 2's Flag.

Figure 9.35 shows an example of a grosgrain ribbon. To make a grosgrain ribbon, begin with a basic rectangle filled with a linear gradient with an angle of about 45°. Draw thin, vertical lines along the width of the rectangle. Duplicate the original layer twice, and then use your Deform/Transform tool to shrink the height of each of the duplicate rectangles to get one thin rectangle along the top edge and one along the bottom edge. Merge the layers and add some shading.

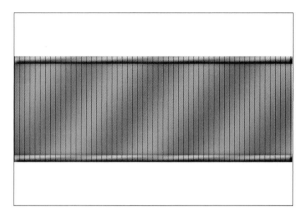

Figure 9.35 A basic grosgrain ribbon.

Fibers

Just about any image editor has a paintbrush tool that can be tweaked for painting fancy lines. In addition to the basic round and square brush tips, you can choose more elaborate shapes. Some of these fancy brush tips are perfect for creating simulated fibers, such as cord or yarn.

Figure 9.36 shows an example of Photoshop Element's Large Starburst brush shape. On the left is a single dab of the brush, showing the shape of the brush tip itself. On the right is some yarn drawn with multiple back-and-forth drags of that brush, with the spacing between brush dabs set to 25%.

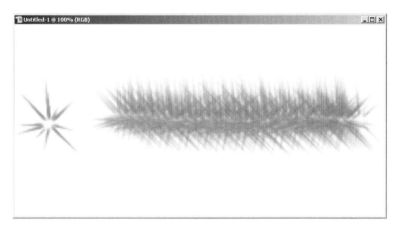

Figure 9.36 Simulated yarn painted with a fancy brush tip.

You can get even more sophisticated effects if your image editor supports brush options that let you vary the brush's color, size, or rotation as you drag. For example, Paint Shop Pro has Brush Variance (available on the Brush Variance palette), PhotoPlus has Brush Options, and Photoshop Elements has More Options (available on the Brush Tool's options bar). Figure 9.37 shows a few examples of fibers created in Paint Shop Pro 8.1 using different colors, brush shapes, and Brush Variance settings.

See your application's manual or Help file for more information on brushes, and then experiment to see the great effects you can create.

Figure 9.37 A few sample fibers.

TIP

If your image editor has a tool that lets you paint with images—such as Paint Shop Pro's Picture Tubes, PhotoImpact's Stamp, or PhotoPlus's Picture Brush—you can use these tools to make realistic-looking cords and ropes. Try spheres or clusters of spheres as the image with which you paint, setting the spacing quite low.

Figure 9.38 shows an example in which Paint Shop Pro's Rope Picture Tube is used to make a gold cord and tassel.

Figure 9.38 A cord and tassel made with Paint Shop Pro's Picture Tube tool.

10

Further Fun with Photos

In Chapter 7, "Advanced Photo Techniques," we looked at some fun things to do with black and white photos. In this chapter, we'll explore some other ways to modify photos to achieve special effects, including combining photos to make montages and panoramas, performing digital facelifts, and using photos to simulate drawings and paintings.

One of the most popular uses of an image editor is the creation of artificial photos, either by combining multiple photos or modifying a single existing photo. In this section, we'll look at a couple ways to combine photos. Later in the chapter, you'll see how to subtly change a portrait—giving the subject a digital facelift—and how to give photos artistic effects.

Compositing Photos

A *composite* is a combination of two or more photos, or photos and non-photographic images. The result looks like an original photo. The simplest case of a composite involves placing a figure from a photo onto a new background.

Isolating the Figure

Let's begin with the photo in Figure 10.1, isolating the young woman from the busy background and creating a new uncluttered background to get the result shown in Figure 10.2.

Figure 10.1 A portrait ready for a new background.

Figure 10.2 The figure placed in its new milieu.

How to isolate the figure from the background will depend in part on your specific image editor. All image editors have a collection of selection tools, and those tools are the first to try. If the background is more or less uniform, you'll probably get good results with the Magic Wand, which creates a selection based on the characteristics of the pixel you click.

Unfortunately, in most cases where you want to isolate a figure from the background, the background is too complex for the Magic Wand to handle. If your image editor has a selection tool that detects edges, use it if the Magic Wand won't do. Here's a list of edge-detecting selection tools in some common image editors:

Digital Image Pro 9
> Edge Finder selection tool

Paint Shop Pro 8.1
> Freehand Selection tool in Edge Seeker, SmartEdge, or Point to Point mode

PhotoImpact XL
> Lasso tool with Snap to Edges selected

PhotoPlus 9
> Magnetic Selection tool

Photoshop Elements 2.0
> Magnetic Lasso tool

The general method with these tools is to drag the tool around the edge of the figure. Then, you can copy the selected figure and paste it onto a new background. Another alternative is to invert the selection, delete the old background, turn off the selection, and add a new background to a new layer below the one containing your isolated figure.

Many image editors also include specialized tools for isolating a figure from a background. These include the Magic Eraser in Photoshop Elements, the Background Eraser in Paint Shop Pro and Photoshop Elements, and Extract in PhotoPlus.

Photoshop Elements' Magic Eraser is probably the simplest of these tools. It's very much like the Magic Wand selection tool, except that instead of creating a selection based on the characteristics of a pixel that you click on, the Magic Eraser erases a group of pixels based on the characteristics of a pixel you click on. Figure 10.3 shows an example of the Magic Eraser in action.

The Background Eraser in both Paint Shop Pro and Photoshop Elements is more sophisticated. With this tool, you set a large brush size and position the center of the brush in an area you want to delete with the edge of the brush overlapping the area you want to keep, as shown in Figure 10.4.

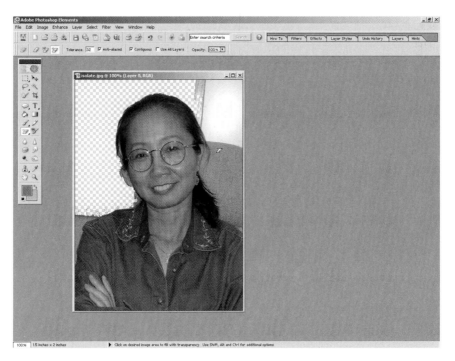

Figure 10.3 Photoshop Elements' Magic Eraser deletes pixels that resemble the one you click.

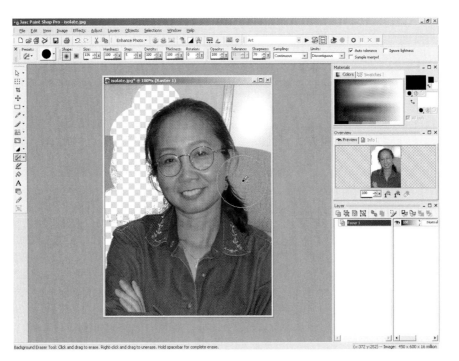

Figure 10.4 Paint Shop Pro's Background Eraser erases the background, leaving only the figure.

PhotoPlus's Edit > Extract command is also a sophisticated edge-detecting background deleter. In this case, you define the edges between the background and the figure, as shown in Figure 10.5.

Then, you fill in the part of the image that you want to keep, as shown in Figure 10.6.

Clicking OK deletes the areas outside the figure, giving the results shown in Figure 10.7.

NOTE

> No matter which of these methods you use, be prepared to do a little clean-up erasing and maybe a bit of cloning. None of these methods is foolproof, and each requires a bit of practice. Once you have some experience with these tools and understand their limitations, you'll find them invaluable.

Another approach is to use masks, quick masks, or editable selections to isolate a figure from a background. We won't examine these here because they're rather complex and vary quite a bit from image editor to image editor. Be sure to consult your editor's manual or Help file to learn more about these powerful tools.

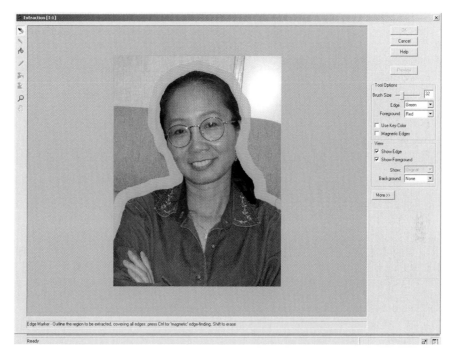

Figure 10.5 Defining the edges in PhotoPlus's Extract mode.

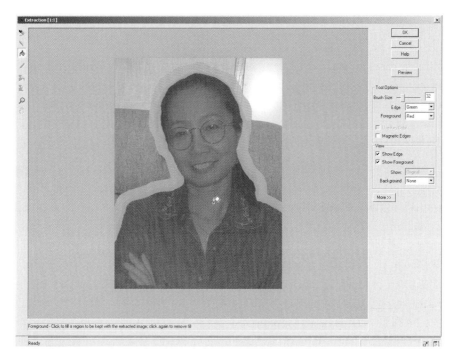

Figure 10.6 Defining the figure.

Figure 10.7 The extracted figure.

The New Background

Once you have the figure isolated, you're ready to add the new background. One possibility is to create a gradient or pattern background. To do this, add a new layer above the isolated figure, and then drag the new layer below the figure layer in the layer stack. With the new layer as the active layer, add a gradient or pattern to the empty layer, as shown in Figure 10.2.

Another possibility is to copy the figure and paste it onto an existing background. Suppose you want to place the isolated figure shown on the left in Figure 10.8 onto the background shown on the right.

Copy the figure and paste it as a new layer onto the background image. You may then need to do a little tweaking, perhaps blurring the background, adjusting the colors and contrast so that the two layers match more closely, and maybe using your Dodge and Burn brushes to add some highlights and shadows to the edges of the figure. When you're done, you'll have results like Figure 10.9.

Figure 10.8 An isolated figure and a separate background.

Figure 10.9 The figure at home in its new locale.

Photo Montage

A *photo montage* combines photos to create an artistic composition, like the one in Figure 10.10. This image was created using the three photos shown in Figure 10.11.

To create this montage, begin with the large background image. Next, copy the kitten image and paste it as a new layer onto the background image. Position the pasted-in photo, resizing it as needed, and then use the Eraser to remove areas you don't want to keep, adjusting the opacity of the Eraser as you go so that the edges gradually fade away. Or, use your application's freehand selection tool ("lasso") to select the area you want to keep. Feather the selection, invert it, and delete the area in the inverted selection. In either case, you'll have something like Figure 10.12.

Figure 10.10 A photo montage.

Figure 10.11 The photos used in the montage.

Figure 10.12 Blending the pasted-in photo with the background.

Follow the same procedure with the next photo, copying it and pasting it as a new layer above the previously pasted-in photo. Delete the areas you don't want, making sure to gradually fade the edges.

Repeat for any other photos you want to add to the montage. Adjust the opacity and blending modes for each of the layers to get the effect you want. Maybe add a pattern to one of the layers. You can also lighten or darken a layer, or adjust the colors or contrast. When you're done, you can merge all the layers together and save the finished image. (You may also want to keep a copy of the layered version in case you want to make changes to it later.)

NOTE

> Some scrappers refer to a photo montage as a *collage*. Technically, a collage is pretty much what you find in a typical scrapbook layout: photos combined with cut and torn paper and other objects. However, a collection of photos that are subtly blended together is a *montage*.
>
> Just to make things even more complicated, montage is also sometimes used to refer to a photo where the colors of the photo are replaced by tiny photos. The Xenofex 2 plug-in filter Stamp produces this type of effect, as does Serif's Montage Plus product.

Creating a Panorama

There are software applications, such as Jasc's Paint Shop Photo Album, that have a built-in facility for creating a panorama by "stitching" together a series of photos. You can also create a panorama from scratch with your image editor without too much extra effort.

You need to start out with two or more photos. First, take a photo at one end of the scene, pivot to take the next shot, then pivot to take the next shot, and so on. The photos should be shot so that there's quite a bit of overlap between adjacent shots (with a 50% overlap ideal). For this example, let's use the two shots of a desert scene shown in Figure 10.13.

Here's how to put the photos together to create a seamless panorama:

1. Open a new image canvas that's large enough to hold both photos side by side. It's a good idea to have some extra vertical space because the photos probably won't line up exactly.

Figure 10.13 Beginning with two separate photos.

Figure 10.14 Pasting in the first photo.

2. Copy the first photo and paste it as a new layer in your new image canvas. Figure 10.14 shows where the first photo is pasted in as a layer over a transparent image canvas. Position the photo as needed.

3. Copy the next photo and paste it as a new layer. Position it as needed. If you need to line the layer up with the previous layer, use a rotation or straightening tool to do so. The result should look like Figure 10.15.

Figure 10.15 Positioning the second photo.

TIP

To help position the pasted-in layer correctly, temporarily reduce the layer's Opacity so you can see the layer below. When you're finished positioning the layer, reset the layer's Opacity to 100.

Another trick to try is to change the upper layer's blending mode to Difference. When the two layers are lined up correctly, the overlapping areas will appear completely black (or, if the layers' colors don't match exactly, a more or less uniform dark shade with perhaps some highlighted edges showing). When the layers are lined up correctly, change the upper layer's blending mode back to Normal.

4. If you're combining more than two photos, repeat step 3 as needed.

5. Use your image editor's eraser tool with a soft brush setting to make the seams between the image layers less sharp. You can also use your cloning tool to edit the seams and to add content if the image canvas shows through along the edges of the image.

6. If necessary, adjust the color, brightness, and contrast of the layers so that they match one another. Then crop your panorama image so that none of the image canvas is left showing. The final result should look like Figure 10.16.

Figure 10.16 The completed panorama.

NOTE

For a full-size panorama, you'd almost certainly want to use a tripod when taking your series of photos, to be sure that the edges of your photos line up precisely. For panoramas that are not full-size—such as those featured in a scrapbook layout—you can probably get away with much less precision, as the example here shows. In this case, handheld shots will probably do fine.

Digital Face-Lift

In this section, we'll use your image editor's warping and cloning tools to return a middle-aged woman to her youth. Begin with a photo like the one in Figure 10.17. We'll give a general outline of the method here. You can adapt this general method for use with the tools provided in your specific image editor.

Figure 10.17 The original photo.

Now for the fountain of youth:

1. Begin by choosing your image editor's warping tool. Choose the mode that lets you push pixels around by dragging, and set the brush size rather large. Then use the large brush to lift the woman's sagging cheeks, as shown in Figure 10.18.

2. Again using a large brush, push the droopy jowls up, as shown in Figure 10.19.

3. Reduce the brush size, and then gently pull up the corners of the mouth just a little, as shown in Figure 10.20.

4. Now for a step many folks forget about: fixing the neck. Go back to a large brush, and then push the neck in a little, as shown in Figure 10.21.

5. Switch to the cloning tool to clone away the wrinkles. Set the opacity of the brush quite low—about 30% or less is fine. Choose a source area close to the wrinkle, and then click on the wrinkle itself. Click multiple times, resampling as needed to gradually soften the wrinkle. Do the same with other wrinkles. As Figure 10.22 shows, you should remember the neck as well as the face.

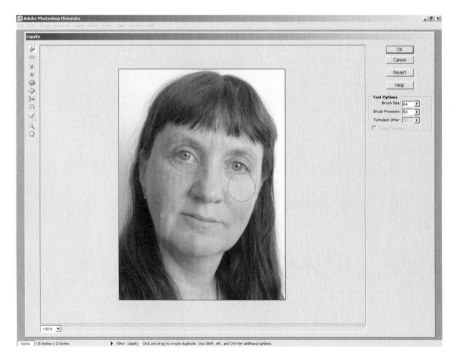

Figure 10.18 Raising the cheeks.

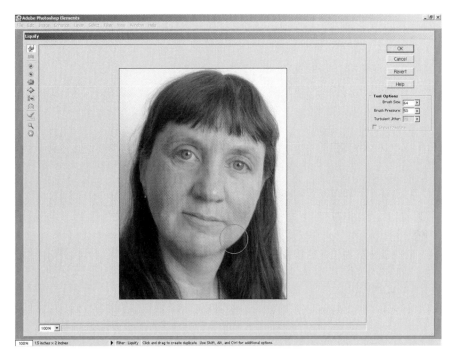

Figure 10.19 Eliminating the jowls.

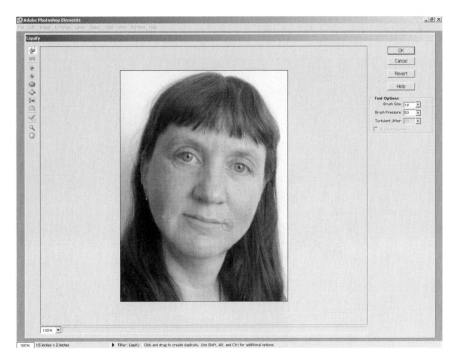

Figure 10.20 Lifting the corners of the mouth.

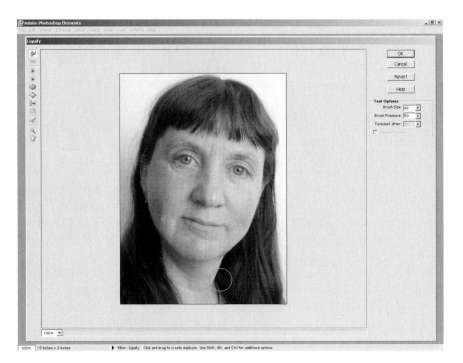

Figure 10.21 Slimming the neck.

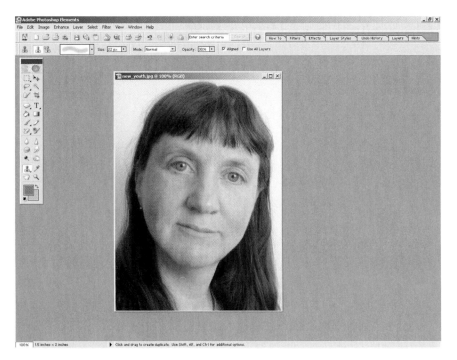

Figure 10.22 Smoothing the wrinkles.

6. As you're working, change the brush size as needed, and dab rather than drag. Keep in mind that the idea here isn't to totally eliminate every line and crease. Even young people have a few lines, and you want to be sure that your edited image looks like a real person, not like a circus clown or a store mannequin. Figure 10.23 shows a side-by-side comparison of the original photo and the completed face-lifted version.

NOTE

Of the image editors we've been examining, probably the two with the best warping tools are Paint Shop Pro, with its Warp Brush, and Photoshop Elements, with its Liquify effect. There are warping tools in the other image editors as well, but their power and responsiveness don't really match Paint Shop Pro's and Photoshop Element's warp tools.

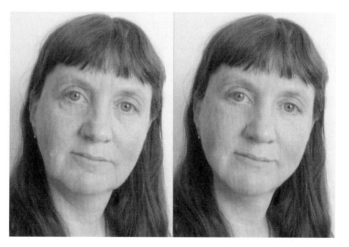

Figure 10.23 Before (left) and after (right).

Drawings and Paintings from Photos

Every image editor includes filters and special effects for transforming photos into drawings and paintings. Some of these produce some stunning effects, but others leave much to be desired. Some plug-in filters, such as Jasc's Virtual Painter, also produce artistic effects. However, you don't need dedicated artistic filters to produce drawings and paintings from your photos. You can also produce great effects by hand.

In this section, we'll go over general outlines for how to achieve these sorts of effects. On the CD, you'll find tailored instructions for how to get these effects using specific image editors, including Paint Shop Pro 8.1, PhotoImpact XL, PhotoPlus 9, and Photoshop Elements 2.0.

NOTE

Unfortunately, Digital Image Pro users cannot use any of the methods outlined here because these methods make use of layer blending modes and dynamically adjustable layer opacity, which Digital Image Pro does not support.

If you use Digital Image Pro, you should try out the various filters in Effects > All Filters to create digital drawings and paintings.

Digital Drawings

Of course, you can create digital drawings purely by hand. With your image editor's painting tools, you can adjust brush settings to get a brush that simulates a pencil, chalk, pastels, or charcoal. It's easy to make a tracing from a photo as well, especially if you have a graphics tablet and stylus. Just add a new layer above your photo, fill the new layer with white, lower the white layer's opacity so you can see the photo beneath, add another layer for the actually tracing, and trace away. Figure 10.24 shows an example in Paint Shop Pro, with the layer structure indicated in the layer palette at the bottom right of the figure. Figure 10.25 shows a sample tracing once the white layer is changed to full opacity.

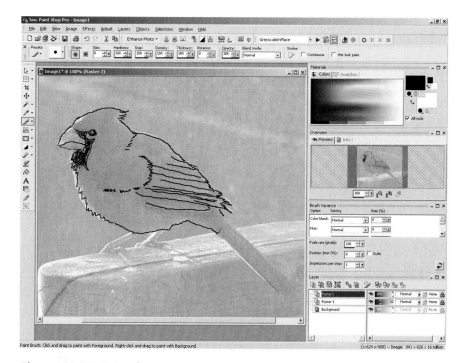

Figure 10.24 Using layers to trace an image.

Figure 10.25 Example of a tracing.

You can also create digital drawings without touching a brush. There are plenty of variations on this technique, but here's one that generally works rather well (although it can't be used in PhotoImpact, which doesn't have a Dodge blending mode):

1. Begin with a color or black and white photo that has a simple, light-colored background, like the one in Figure 10.26. If it's a color photo, convert it to grayscale or use channel mixing to make a black and white version. You'll usually get the best results if you increase the contrast, as shown in Figure 10.27.

2. Duplicate the photo layer. Make this layer a negative version of your original image and set the layer's blending mode to Dodge. The image looks almost completely white, with perhaps some black also showing.

3. Use Gaussian blur set to a value somewhere between 3 and 10. The image will look like Figure 10.28. If you like this look as is, skip to step 6.

4. To add some pencil markings to your sketch, duplicate the bottom layer again. On your new middle layer, add some noise.

Figure 10.26 The original photo.

Figure 10.27 A higher-contrast version.

Figure 10.28 Blurring the negative brings out the edges.

5. Set the layer's blending mode to Darken. Then use a motion blur with the angle of the blur set somewhere between 45 and 55, with the intensity of the blur set to whatever value gives you the effect you want. The result will look like Figure 10.29.

6. Optional: Merge the layers, and then adjust the brightness and contrast with Levels or Curves.

Figure 10.29 Pencil marks added.

Digital Paintings

Your image editor probably includes a host of special effects that can be applied to a photo to create painting-like variations. You can also create your own painting-from-photos effects with commands that add or remove noise, affect edges, and/or blur your image. Here's an example, starting with the photo in Figure 10.30. This example was done in PhotoPlus, but you can adapt this method for use with just about any image editor.

1. Open your photo image. (Even improperly exposed or blurry photos can work with this technique.)

Figure 10.30 The original photo.

2. Duplicate the Background layer twice. Turn off the visibility of the top layer for now, and make the middle layer the active layer. Use a command that emphasizes the dark areas of your image, such as PhotoPlus's Effects > Other > Minimum. Set the blending mode to Dissolve and the opacity to 50 or less. The result looks like Figure 10.31.

3. Make the top layer visible and active. Set the blending mode to Dodge and set the opacity quite low (25 or less). This brightens the image, as shown in Figure 10.32. Your painting is then complete.

4. Optional: If you like, you can also blur the Background layer. Make the Background layer the active layer and apply a blur command, such as PhotoPlus's Effects > Blur > Median.

This is just one simple example. Try other blur, noise reduction, and edge-detecting commands alone or in combination to produce other painting-like effects. Be sure to try different blending modes and opacities when you combine different layers to produce your digital paintings.

Figure 10.31 Dissolving a layer with emphasized dark areas into the blurred layer.

Figure 10.32 Brightening the image with the Dodge blending mode.

TIP

You're not limited to modifying photos to create digital paintings, of course. You can also create your digital paintings completely by hand. Most image editors have a collection of paintbrush shapes, many of which mimic physical drawing and painting tools. Also, explore some of the retouching tools, especially those that smudge pixels together or push them around, such as Paint Shop Pro's Smudge and Push brushes. If you have experience with physical painting—or if you're just feeling adventurous—give it a try, perhaps using a photo as your model.

Using Modified Photos in Layouts

Modifying your photos to create composites, panoramas, drawings, and paintings is fun and yields some interesting results, but how would you, the digital scrapper, use these modified photos in your layouts? Figures 10.33 through 10.35 show some examples. Use these as a springboard for your own creations.

Figure 10.33 A layout featuring a montage by Samuel Kordik.

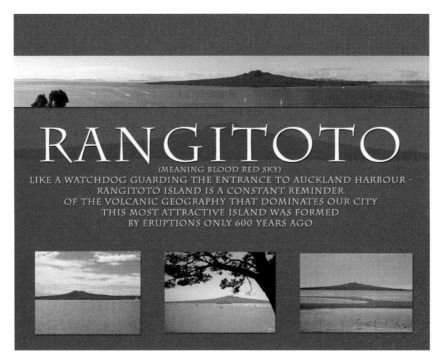

Figure 10.34 A layout featuring a panorama by Lauren Bavin.

Figure 10.35 A layout featuring a digital drawing by Lori J. Davis.

A

Resources

The resources listed here are just the beginning. Be sure to check online search engines for more digital scrapbooking resources. Keep in mind that things on the Web are constantly changing, so some of the links listed below may no longer be active.

The Authors' Web Sites

Here are the Web sites of this book's authors, along with an online learning site where Sally and Lori teach digital scrapbooking classes.

Dizteq by Sally Beacham

www.dizteq.com

Resources, tutorials, tools, and recommendations for Photoshop-compatible plug-in filters. In addition, you'll find some resources for Paint Shop Pro and Xara X as well as links to great sites.

Lori's Web Graphics by Lori J. Davis

loriweb.pair.com

Web graphics for sure, but also tutorials and goodies for digital scrappers who want to print their creations.

LVS Online

www.lvsonline.com

There are several places online where you can take scrapbook-related courses, and LVS Online is one of the best. Sally teaches courses with Cindi Bisson on scrapbook design, and Sally and Lori teach a class on creating digital scrapbook elements. Ron Lacey's courses on digital photography as well as several courses on image editors, such as Paint Shop Pro and PhotoImpact, are also of interest to scrappers.

Scrapbooking Magazines

There are many, many scrapbooking magazines, and by the time you read this there could very well be many more. Check out the Crafts offerings in the periodicals section of your local bookstore or crafts store for the latest in scrapbook magazines. Many magazines have Web sites where you can read articles, access resources, and even submit your work for possible publication. Here are some examples:

Creating Keepsakes
www.creatingkeepsakes.com

Memory Makers
www.memorymakersmagazine.com

Simple Scrapbooks
www.simplescrapbooksmag.com

Digital Scrapbooking Web Sites and Newsgroups

There are dozens of online sites where scrappers can meet, share their ideas, ask questions, and show off their layouts. Here are a few to get you started:

Digital Scrapbook Place
www.digitalscrapbookplace.com

Pages of the Heart
www.pagesoftheheart.net

Scrapbook Bytes
www.scrapbook-bytes.com

Computer Scrapping
groups.yahoo.com/group/computer-scrapping

Computer Scrapping Elements 2
groups.yahoo.com/group/computerscrappingelements2

Digital Scrapbooking at Annexcafe
news:annexcafe.hobbies.digital.scrapbook

General Scrapbooking Web Sites

The sites below are general scrapping sites, with an emphasis on paper scrapping:

Scrapbook.com
www.scrapbook.com

Scrapbooking.com
www.scrapbooking.com

ScrapbookAddict
www.scrapbookaddict.com

Scrapping Arts
www.scrappingarts.com

Scrapjazz
www.scrapjazz.com

Scrapbook Designers

There are probably hundreds and hundreds of scrapbook designers active on the Web. Here's information on the designers who contributed kits or templates to the book's CD, along with the sites of the other designers who contributed examples for this book.

Lauren Bavin

Lauren Bavin is a stay-at-home mother of three living in Auckland, New Zealand. She became passionate about digital scrapbooking after getting her first digital camera nearly two years ago, and gradually has developed into a paper-style digital scrapbooker. She's been a designer for Pages of the Heart, Elemental, and now is part of Team Digital at www.digitalscrapbookplace.com. She's been published in several scrapbook magazines including *Memory Makers*, *Scrapbook Memories*, and *PaperKuts*. Her page kits are currently for sale at both www.digitalscrapbookplace.com and www.pagesoftheheart.com.

Angela M. Cable

Angela M. Cable, www.neocognition.com, is a Web designer, artist, and amateur photographer. Angela has been the technical editor for several publications, including this book. Angela lives in Wyoming with her loving fur-face, C.C.

Kim Liddiard

Kim Liddiard, a designer for Digital Scrapbook Place, creates realistic layout designs for digital scrapbooking. Visit her Web site at The Creative Pixel (www.thecreativepixel.com). In addition to downloadable digital scrapbook art, she has published a CD of Page Kits and Instant Layouts called "Creative Pixels, Vol. 1 - a work of heART!"

Margie Lundy

Margie Lundy has been a digital scrapbooker since 2001 and has been published in the following magazines: *Creaking Keepsakes*, *Simple Scrapbooks*, *Memory Makers*, *PaperKuts*, and *Ivy Cottage Creations*, as well as various idea books, special issues, and Web sites. She started the computer-scrapping Yahoo e-mail group at www.computer-scrapping.com and has been a design team member for two large Web sites. She co-founded DigitalScrapbookPlace.com, which offers community, education, and products for the digital scrapbooker.

Janice "Maya" Dye-Szucs

Janice "Maya" Dye-Szucs has a career history that includes advertising and Web design. She is a Design Team Member at Scrapbook-Bytes.com, where her most recent layouts are available for viewing in her gallery. You can also visit her site at www.scrapbookgraphics.com.

Tracy Pori

Tracy Pori is a freelance instructional writer for Photoshop, Paint Shop Pro, and Adobe Elements in the internationally-distributed *Digital Photography Techniques* magazine and has a graphic and Web design business in beautiful Southern Oregon. She also has digital scrapbook elements for sale at www.digitalartresources.com/scrapbook.htm. You can contact Tracy at digitalartresources@yahoo.com.

Jenna Robertson

Jenna Robertson, a designer for Digital Scrapbook Place, has been scrapping for several years, finally combining her love of scrapping and Paint Shop Pro in 2001.

Other Designers of Layouts Featured in the Book

Listed below are designers who contributed to the examples in the book, along with their Web sites.

- Jenny Bamford-Perkins

  www.scrappingarts.com

  www.ourvintageshoppe.com

- Amanda Behrmann

  www.digitalscrapbookplace.com

- Cindi Bisson

  www.fatcatcreations.info

- Kristin Cronin-Barrow

  Gallery at www.digitalscrapbookplace.com

- Pat Goettels

  Pat is a 100% paper scrapper and not online.

- Jeri Ingalls

  www.littlehousetwo.homestead.com/indexscrapbook.html

- Samuel Kordik

  Gallery at www.digitalscrapbookplace.com

Image Editor and Photo Album Manufacturers

Serious scrappers need an image editor for creating layouts and maybe even creating their own elements. You don't need to spend US$600 on Adobe Photoshop for high-quality. Image editors in the US$100 range are more than adequate. Listed below are the manufacturers of some of the most popular, affordable image editors. These software producers also have other applications that can be useful to the digital scrapper.

Adobe

www.adobe.com

Makers of Photoshop, Photoshop Elements, and Adobe Photo Album.

Jasc Software, Inc.

www.jasc.com

Makers of Paint Shop Pro, Paint Shop Photo Album, and Animation Shop.

Microsoft

www.microsoft.com

Maker of Digital Image Pro.

Serif

www.serif.com

Makers of PhotoPlus, DrawPlus, PagePlus, and more.

Ulead

www.ulead.com

Makers of PhotoImpact, Photo Explorer, PictureShow, and more.

Digital Camera, Printer, and Scanner Web Sites

Here are a few of the largest and best manufacturers of digital cameras, printers, and scanners:

Canon
www.canon.com

Epson
www.epson.com

Fujifilm
www.fujifilm.com

HP
www.hp.com

Kodak
www.kodak.com

Minolta
www.minolta.com

Nikon
www.nikon.com

Pentax
www.pentax.com

Plug-ins and Utilities

There are zillions of great plug-ins. Here's just a sampling of sources to get you started. Be warned: Plug-in collecting can be quite addictive.

Alien Skin Software

www.alienskin.com

Makers of Eye Candy 4000, Eye Candy 5 Textures, Xenofex 2, Splat!, and Image Doctor. Alien Skin's Eye Candy and Xenofex plug-in filters are great for creating effects for text, embellishments, and more. Splat! is great for creating borders, edges, frames, and textures. Image Doctor is a set of filters for photo correction. Demos of the Eye Candy filters, Xenofex, and Splat! are included on the book's CD.

AmphiSoft

photoshop.msk.ru/as

Makers of several fine freeware and shareware filters. Demos and a few freebies are included on the book's CD.

Auto FX

www.autofx.com

Makers of many high-quality plug-in filters. Those of particular interest to scrappers are filters in their DreamSuite series and Photo/Graphic Edges. In addition to their commercial filters, they offer a pair of free filter sets: DreamSuite Dreamy Photo and DreamSuite Mosaic. Demos of DreamSuite Series One and Photo/Graphic Edges are included on the book's CD.

AV Bros.

www.avbros.com

Makers of Page Curl, Puzzle Pro, and Colorist. Page Curl provides two very realistic effects: a turning page effect (Page Curl) and a folding page effect (Page Fold). Puzzle Pro helps you create jigsaw puzzle effects, and it also produces various other high-quality image effects. Colorist is a small, handy standalone program that lets you choose a color and then get its RGB, HSB, and Hex values using the program's color wheel or a large library of named colors. Demos of each of these are included on the book's CD.

Color Schemer

www.colorschemer.com

Makers of Color Schemer, an easy-to-use color matching application that will help you select creative color schemes. A demo is included on the book's CD.

LumaPix

www.lumapix.com

Makers of FotoFusion, a tool for creating collages and scrapbook pages. Many scrappers love this application. A demo is included on the book's CD.

namesuppressed

www.namesuppressed.com

Tone your digital photos, create plaid patterns, and add dreamy effects with the shareware plug-in filters from namesuppressed: Autochromatic, Plaid Lite, and Softener (demos are included on the book's CD). Many scrappers are particularly fond of Plaid Lite, which takes colors from an image and uses those colors to create beautiful plaid patterns.

Redfield Plugins

www.redfieldplugins.com

You can find many wonderful plug-ins—some free and some at a modest price—at Redfield Plugins. Redfield's plug-ins are great for creating texturing and similar effects. A nice sampling is included on the book's CD.

The Plugin Site

www.thepluginsite.com

Harry Heim's The Plugin Site is a great place for information on plug-ins and for lots and lots of great filters, both by Harry and others. Among Harry's fine filters and utilities are ColorWasher and FocalBlade (for photo correction and enhancement), PhotoFreebies (a set of free filters for photo manipulation), and Edge and Frame Galaxy (a great utility for adding decorative edges and colored frames to images). PhotoFreebies and demos of ColorWasher, FocalBlade, and Edge and Frame Galaxy are included on the book's CD.

Virtual Painter

www.livecraft.com/vp.htm

www.virtualpainter.com

Virtual Painter, available as either a standalone application or a plug-in filter, turns your favorite digital photos into realistic-looking paintings, in any of several different styles. A demo is included on the book's CD.

Virtual Painter is offering our readers a $10 discount on any full version of Virtual Painter 4. For details, go to the Course Technology Web site at www.courseptr.com.

Fonts

Every scrapbooker needs at least a few more fonts than what you'll find as standards for your operating system. Here's a sampling of sources for free and commercial fonts. Search online and you'll find many more.

Astigmatic One Eye Typographic Institute

www.astigmatic.com

Designers of a large collection of gorgeous commercial and free fonts.

House of Lime

www.houseoflime.com

Source of many fine fonts and dingbats, some specifically designed with scrappers in mind. Samples are included on the book's CD.

Larabie Fonts

www.larabiefonts.com

Ray Larabie's fonts are some of the best around. Check out his extensive collections of free and commercial fonts. Samples are included on the book's CD.

The Dingbat Pages

www.dingbatpages.com

Extensive compendium of dingbat fonts from a variety of designers. Fonts are available as freeware, shareware, guiltware, charityware, and postcardware.

Typadelic Fonts

www.typadelic.com

Beautiful fonts—from grungy to lovely—from font designer Ronna Penner. Samples are included on the book's CD.

Clip Art

Clip art is ready-made line art and photos that you can use in your designs. You probably have some already, bundled with your word processor, office suite, image editor, or other applications. Here are a few more commercial sources.

Dover

www.doverpublications.com

Dover Publications offers numerous clip art collections, many of them of particular interest to scrappers. A few samples are included on the book's CD.

Hemera

www.hemera.com

Hemera offers a distinct type of clip art: photo objects. The samplers included on the book's CD include both standard clip art and photo objects.

Online Photo Sharing and Printing

There are many excellent sites where you can share your photos with others, order prints, and maybe even create a hardcover book of your photos or layouts. Here are a few examples:

Ofoto
www.ofoto.com

Shutterfly
www.shutterfly.com

Snapfish
www.snapfish.com

Another service that offers hardcover binding of layouts is Bound 2 Remember (www.bound2remember.com).

Web Hosts

If you'd like to have your own Web site without spending a lot of money, here are a couple places to check out:

Angelfire
www.angelfire.com

Tripod
www.tripod.com

To find other possibilities, go to any online search engine and search on "web host".

General Photography and Scanning-Related Web Sites

Chances are that if you're a scrapper, you're also an amateur photographer (or maybe even a pro). To learn more about photography and scanning, begin with these helpful sites.

Digital Photography Review

www.dpreview.com

Plenty of reviews of cameras and related hardware along with informative articles, instructional material, and much more.

Scan Tips

www.scantips.com

Wayne Fulton's classic fact-filled site on, you guessed it, tips about scanning.

Index

U

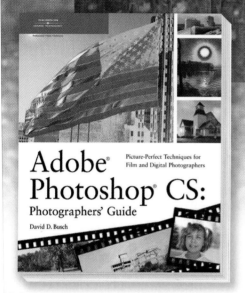